ANOTHER SLICE OF PI

ROLAND BYRD

ANOTHER SLICE OF PI

Publications

Copyrights © 2015 Roland Byrd.

All rights reserved. No part of this book may be scanned, or distributed in any printed or electronic form without permission. Please do not participate in or encourage piracy of copyrighted materials in violation of the authors' rights.

Purchase only authorized editions

This book is available at special quantity discounts for bulk purchase for sales promotions, premiums, fundraising, and educational needs. For details email Roland@RolandByrd.com.

ISBN 13: 978-1-940324-11-1

ISBN 10: 1940324111

Neither the author nor the publisher is engaged in rendering professional advice or services to the individual reader. The ideas, procedures, and suggestions contained in this book are not intended as a substitute for consulting with your physician or counselor. All matters regarding your health require medical supervision. Neither the author nor the publisher shall be liable or responsible for any loss or damage allegedly arising from any information or suggestions in this book.

Contents

Introduction 1
Part 1: Transformations 3
Part 2: Health & Fitness 279

Dedication

This book is dedicated to you. You're the reason I write. You're the reason I'm doing my best to leave a positive mark on this world.
    Roland

Introduction

There was a time when I hated myself. I thought I was worthless, a waste of flesh. I felt like the world, and my family would be better off without me. I didn't believe I was worthy of love or mercy. I was so caught up in my own misery that I couldn't empathize with others. I couldn't see past my own pain, so how could I truly open my eyes and heart to others?

I hated the person I'd become but believed I was doomed to be that man, that there was nothing I could do about it. The thought of personal transformation was as alien to me as the concept of freedom to one born into captivity. You might hear about it, you might even dream of it, but you don't believe it's possible. Not deep in your heart where it matters.

I lived nearly 36 years of my life that way. Wanting to be more, dreaming of being more—of being better, but unable to believe it was possible.

Then I had an awakening. I hit the lowest point in my life. All my flawed beliefs and behaviors caught up with me. Everything crashed and burned. It was like my life disintegrated while I watched, helpless...

As I fought to pick up the pieces and rebuild my life, I finally got it. I could choose my life. The state of my life, all the things that happened were results of my choices. And I could make better choices. I might not be able to choose everything that happens but I could always choose how I responded to it, how I internalized it. Like it or not, I finally understood this truth; We are all completely accountable for the state of our lives. We all choose the path our lives take.

That meant that if I wanted to and I was committed to the process, I could change my life. I could change myself!

That started my path of Personal Transformation. Since then I've reinvented myself, become a better man. I'm dedicated to growth, change, and helping others. Sure there are still rough spots, things I'm working on. There always will be. And I'll spend the rest of my life learning, growing, and passing on that knowledge.

As part of my quest to help others learn and grow into the best version of themselves, I started a blog over 4 years ago. I've published over 173 blog posts in that time. This book, Another Slice of Pi, contains nearly all of those posts in an easy to read format. Who knows, they might just help you grow into a better version of yourself.

Always Remember,

You are The Master of Your Destiny!

Roland

Part 1:
Transformations

Imperfect

I'm an imperfect man in an imperfect world. I've made many mistakes, some of them life-altering.

But I finally got it!

Perfection doesn't come from doing everything right all of the time. Perfection is accepting our imperfections, learning from our mistakes, and doing our best to help others through the often confusing thing we call life.

I believe people should pass on their knowledge to others who are on the same path.

I welcome you to my imperfect attempt to share the knowledge I've gained through my life.

Part 1: Transformations

Empathy

Empathy is something that comes easy to some and is harder for others. Regretfully, there was a time in my life when I didn't comprehend empathy. I had a vague idea what the word meant but I just didn't "get it".

Over the past few years I've come to understand what empathy is and how it helps in our lives though. And I'm glad I have.

After all, can you have a true connection with others when you fail to understand—or try to—what they're going through, what they've been through, or the impact your actions could have on them?

I couldn't. I wasn't sure how to "empathize" past the end of my nose. And my relationships showed it.

Thankfully we humans can change! It took awhile but I did start to "get it". As I learn how to empathize more, I have a better understanding of those around me and my relationships grow deeper and more meaningful.

So I wanted to share the best definition of Empathy I've read. Maybe it will help you "get it" too. Or maybe you already have empathy down pat. Either way, this is a great quote.

By Steven R. Covey—From *Principle Centered Leadership*.

"Empathy is the ability to comprehend with accuracy the precise thoughts and motivations of other people in such a way that they would say; 'Yes, that is exactly where I am coming from.'

"Empathy is not the capacity to feel the same way someone else feels.

"Empathy is not acting in a tender, understanding manner.

"Empathy is the ultimate anger antidote.

"Empathy is the ability to visualize the consequences, good and bad, of your behavior.

"Empathy is the ability to conceptualize the impact of what you do on yourself and on the other person, and to feel appropriate and genuine sorrow and regret without labeling yourself as inherently bad."

Part 1: Transformations

Do You Know The Power in a Single Voice?

I was driving the other day when it hit me. Every person on this planet has nearly limitless potential. But almost all of them are trapped in their own small version of reality. I felt overpowering hope and joy at the thought of the changes that could come to pass if even a fraction of these people would realize the beauty of their creation and their potential.

A lot of people don't try because they think a single voice can't make a difference. But a single voice can start an avalanche. A single voice can start or stop a riot. A single voice can open the front of the bus to a race of people. There *is power* in a single voice—the power to create *and* the power to destroy. But the voice *has to be used* or the power withers and dies.

And we never know who that voice might be until we open our mouths and discover it within us.

"Most people spend their life waiting for a miracle to happen. Other people just decide to be the Miracle."—Martin Latulippe

Why Life by Design?

I thought I'd fill you in on why I chose the name "Your Blueprint, Life by Design" for my book and "Life by Design" for this blog.

The first part; *Your Blueprint* is probably easy to guess. Your Blueprint is the template for your life. My Blueprint is the template for my life. We all have a blueprint and that Blueprint is responsible for most of the results we get in life.

But *what if you aren't happy with the results you're getting?*

That's where Life by Design comes in.

Understand that many things shape your Blueprint. Things like the movies and shows you watch, the music you listen to, things people you care for and trust say around you, things you read, even things you hear or see without knowing it... All of these leave an imprint. That means most people go through life with a Blueprint that's like a patch-work quilt of beliefs they picked up along the way.

There is no rhyme or reason to their Blueprint. This can lead to interesting behavior and unwanted results.

Your beliefs might be empowering, crippling, or a mixture. But they are Your Blueprint.

The great news is this. If you are unhappy with any part of your life, you can re-design it by deliberately crafting a new section in Your Blueprint. That gives you the power to shape your life the way you want.

In short, it empowers you to live a Life by Design. :-)

Part 1: Transformations

Do You Really Want Success?

Have you ever noticed that many people are great at talking about how much they *want to change* but not so great at doing anything about it? They have opportunities to make a difference in their lives...but they just watch them sail on by.

Imagine you see a person sitting on the side of the road, soaking up the sun. They have a sign out that reads, "Florida or Bust!" and you happen to be driving to Florida. So you pull over and offer them a ride.

"No thank you." They reply. And close their eyes.

"But your sign says, 'Florida or Bust' and I'm offering you a ride." You say.

They slowly open their eyes, look at their sign, and say, "Why...so it does." They scratch their head. "Yep. 'Florida or Bust!' Right there plain as day." Then they shrug.

"So...do you want a ride?" You ask in exasperation.

"Nope. Not today." Then they look at you and wink. "Come back tomorrow. I'll be ready for that ride then. Just not today." Then they turn away from you as if you were never there.

That's what many people are like when it comes to doing anything that will change their lives. They want it. They prepare for it. But when push comes to shove, they sit down and shrug, "Not Today."

I hope you're not that type of person. I hope you'll take action on your dreams and do what it takes to bring them

Another Slice of Pi

to reality. I hope you believe in yourself and that you want change enough to actually do something about it!

It might happen slower than you want or faster than you want. There's no way of knowing the timeframe up front. But I can promise this, unless you do something, you'll just sit by the side of the road and watch your dreams pass by.

Realize your dreams or not. It's your choice.

Part 1: Transformations

Stream of Consciousness

This is a fun exercise. Take a piece of paper—or a word processor—and just start writing. It's called a stream of consciousness exercise. It can feel awkward at first, but if you just go with it you'll soon find that some remarkable things emerge.

I'll do it now.

Ok. This feels scary because I'm committed top posting whatever I write. But that's ok. I think you'll forgive me if it's a bit odd. After all, I've been known to be a bit eccentric. J

The other day I was driving through town trying to find a client's location when I gut stumped. I was stumped because my GPS showed I was at the address when I obviously wasn't. I was confused at first but then figured out that my GPS had taking me to the farthest south address on the N-S road I was on and called that good.

That got me thinking about how sometimes we humans trust technology—or other people more than we trust ourselves. And that's sad. After all, we have this remarkable gut radar that gives us clues about what we're doing and if it's helpful or harmful to us.

Haven't you ever just "known" that something good was going to happen? Or had a feeling of dread that steered you away from an activity that seemed harmless otherwise?

I know I have. In fact I remember one time that is poignant.

Another Slice of Pi

I was at a park and my daughter—then about five—disappeared. I looked around and she was nowhere. But I knew I had to find her, "Right Away!"

Without thinking about it I ran around the edge of the pavilion just in time to see her feet vanish over the edge of a dunking tank! I sprinted over and grabbed her out of the water within seconds. And if I hadn't been there she would have probably drowned because there was no ladder inside of the tank!

I'm so grateful I listened to the feeling that helped me and saved my daughter's life!

And I encourage you to listen to your gut too. Call it the Holy Ghost. Call it your gut. Call it being in tune with the universe. Whatever you decide to call it, it's real and it will help guide you in your life if you let it.

And that, my friends, is a stream of consciousness exercise. Try it sometime. You might be surprised at what it does for you.

Part 1: Transformations

Possibilities

I woke this morning with a cloud of possibilities spinning in my head. I felt like everything is possible, like I can do anything I decide to do.

Have you ever felt that way?

It's an empowering feeling. It overwhelms the senses and fills you with energy. The world is at your fingertips!

All you have to do is *act!*

You have to *move your feet* in the direction of your dream.

Times like this happen a lot when you're aligned with your true passion. There isn't any, "Do I have to?" Instead it's, "Wow! Look what I get to do today!"

Now I've had times when I tried to align myself with what "I thought" should be my passion. As I'm sure you know…that didn't work so well. I ended up being in a battle with myself where I tried and tried to convince myself to do things—so my pseudo-dream would happen.

But when you're aligned with your passion, when your dream is real; that's when the real magic happens! Nothing stops you!

Why?

Because you wake up filled with possibility! You feel fire in your heart and tingling in your veins. You can't wait to get started!

Another Slice of Pi

I have had so many miracles happen in my life when I'm aligned with my true passion. There are countless things that have happened, that I was promised, "would never happen" by people in the know. I've made changes in myself that I was told were "impossible" and I've empowered others to change too.

But these things only happen when I'm on the right path.

I don't know what your path is. That's for you to discover. I know you have a true passion though. And I can promise you this; If you'll take the time to figure out your true passion, and use it to help others, you'll discover that *nothing holds you back!*

Part 1: Transformations

Play it safe

Do You Play It Safe on Your Quest for Your Dreams?

I've been told that I have "grandiose" dreams; that I'm irrational in the outcomes I desire and the methods I use. I've also been told to "just *BE* normal."

To Play it Safe...

That was hard for me to accept. So I chose to ignore it.

I'm actively improving myself. I've studied diligently over the past three years. I've learned ways to improve myself and develop self-worth. By all accounts I've made tremendous changes in my life and my thought processes, all of which have been for my good.

So when it comes to playing small or being normal, I ask, "Who am I hurting by dreaming on a 'grandiose' scale?"

If I dream small I'll get small results.

Now that's the "normal" thing to do. And if that's normal, I want nothing to do with it! I want to be extraordinary. After all, every human being who's ever lived has the ability to be extraordinary. So why should I sell myself short? I want extraordinary results.

I desire to help as many people as I can live healthier and happier lives. According to some, this is irrational thinking. But that smacks of, "who am I to make a difference?" or, "keep your head down and get back in line."

I reject these outright.

Instead I ask, "Who am I, if I fail to make a difference?"

Power of Choice

Do You Exercise Your Power of Choice?

Whether you do—or not—has a great impact on the quality of your life. For example, let's take being a Victim & having a Victim Mentality.

These two things may seem related, but in fact they are worlds apart. You can be a victim without having a victim mentality and you can have a victim mentality without being a victim.

I think defining Victim and Victim Mentality might help.
From Merriam-Webster

Victim: One that is injured, destroyed, or sacrificed under any of various conditions <a *victim* of cancer> <a *victim* of the auto crash> <a murder *victim*>

One that is subjected to oppression, hardship, or mistreatment <a frequent *victim* of political attacks>

Mentality: Mode or way of thought: outlook <the imperialist *mentality* of the nineteenth century — John Davies>

Victim Mentality: One who's mode or way of thought is as if they are a victim. (That's my definition.)

It's true that sometimes crappy things happen. I'm sure something happened to in your life that was outside your control and that harmed you in some way. You were thus a "Victim" of that event.

But what did you do with it then?
That's what makes the difference!

Part 1: Transformations

If you chose to keep focusing on the event and how it harmed you, then you were exhibiting a "Victim Mentality." In short you were choosing to let the event continue to hurt you.

If you chose to seek healing and to do whatever was necessary to continue, despite the crappy thing that happened, then you were showing a success minded mentality.

Remember it's normal to feel emotions about something or someone that hurt you. It's normal to mourn a loss. Those are healthy paths to healing. When you focus on those feelings and continually think about the event that fostered them... That is like digging a hole in your heart. It slows and can even stop the healing process.

I'll give an example from my life:

I had some really crappy things happen to me as a kid. I was the "Victim" in these things. And I chose to remain the victim well into my adulthood. I used the things that happened to me as excuses for things I did. I used them to justify my depression. I felt like my life was out of my control, like I was a marionette in some cosmic joke.

It wasn't until I learned to take accountability for my thoughts and actions that my depression went away. It was only when I realized I could choose how I responded to the events in my life, that I felt true freedom for the first time.

You can choose! No one can ever take that away from you!

There are also people who choose to have the victim mentality about everything. If they are angry, it's someone else's fault. If they are late for work, it's someone else's fault. If they are too fat or too thin, it's someone else's fault. If they drank too much it was because the Bartender didn't cut them off. Etc.

These people must feel like Ping-Pong balls bouncing through life. They have no direction and—in their minds—zero control of their life.

Why would they choose that?

Because being a victim of their life lets them off the hook. It allows them to say, "Hey...I couldn't help it." Or, "It's because of how I was raised." Maybe even, "If you wouldn't do that I wouldn't have to punish you all the time."

Being in a victim state of mind gives them the illusion of no accountability. And believe it or not, that appeals to a lot of people.

There are many problems with living in a victim state of mind—enough to easily fill a book. So I'm going to finish by touching on one aspect.

Success and the Victim Mentality are like oil and water. They just don't mix. If you want success in your life—and I'm talking about genuine success, the kind that permeates your entire life—you have to release the victim mentality. You must take accountability for your life and realize that all of your actions produce results. If you aren't happy with the results... then try different actions!

And please remember: No matter what happens to you, no matter what has happened to you, *you always have the power to choose your response!*

Part 1: Transformations

A Secret

I'm going to let you in on a secret.

When I sit down to write these posts I only have a vague idea what it's going to say in the end. I just have an itching in my brain that says, "Write about this!"

So I do.

Sometimes it's a concept. Sometimes it's a title. Sometimes it's just the urge to write. But no matter what, I always shoot for quality content. I want you to get what you're paying for!

Oh wait, you're not paying. :)

Well hang that! I want you to get much, much more than you're paying for. My desire is that you'll read my blog and think, "Wow! That's GREAT!", that you'll come away a little better or wiser person than you were when you stopped by, and that you'll *tell your friends... ;-)*

Another Slice of Pi

Are You Feeling...Lucky?

Have you ever watched someone roll by in your dream car and thought, "What a lucky $%@$#%!"? Or maybe they have the home you want, the job you want, or the simple life you yearn for.

It doesn't matter what it is. Just take a moment and think about how you feel when someone is—in your perception—better off than you?

Do you curse your luck while bemoaning theirs?

If not GREAT!

If so, do you really think that helps?

What is luck anyway? Is it totally random events that fall into place for some people but not for others? Or, and this is more sinister...Is it really *the Intersection of Preparation and Opportunity?*

Ouch, that means accountability. Many people shy away from accountability.

Are you one of the accountability impaired? Or do you have the power to shape your own destiny?

I know which I choose!

Take a star athlete. When they make a "Lucky" game winning shot, is it a random event? Or is it the result of years spent honing their skills?

Some people might say, "Yeah, but that's different..."

Really? How?

Part 1: Transformations

Would that same athlete make the "Lucky" game winning shot if they never practiced? If they never practiced, would they be a star?

But those things are often called "Luck".

Remember, a person with average talent and an extraordinary work ethic almost always surpasses someone with extraordinary talent and no work ethic.

Your talents might be average, they might be extraordinary. But how is your passion to succeed? How is your work ethic? Those are key ingredients to luck.

Ask yourself this, "Am I willing to *roll up my sleeves* and *prepare myself* for the next opportunity that comes my way?"

Are you ready to be Lucky?

Go ahead and do it. I dare you!

Then the next time someone asks you, "Are you feeling lucky?" You can say, "HECK YEAH!"

Prepare for Success!

Are You Prepared for Success?

The other morning I was on my way to a client's when I thought I'd stop by a fast food joint for breakfast.

I drove by one of the "Big Two" national chains. There were about twenty cars in line. So I continued to the one across the street. There weren't any cars there and I thought, "I'll give them some business." After all, they are a major chain and I like their food too.

I went inside.

The lobby was empty. I walked to the counter. No food in sight, not a morsel. There wasn't even a person at the counter. Someone *was* in back washing dishes. She turned and looked at me, then went back to washing the dishes.

I waited...

A minute, two. No one came to the counter or acknowledged my presence. So I shrugged and left.

Then I drove to the Major Chain across the way and got my food in just a few minutes.

What's my point in telling you this?

Expectation, Preparation, and Success.

The first restaurant obviously expected high traffic during peak breakfast hours, they prepared for it and I'm going to hallucinate that they had a financially successful morning. In fact, they are usually busy.

Part 1: Transformations

The other restaurant—though I've seen their chain going head to head with the other one in many cities—obviously didn't expect to be busy. And they weren't. They had—I imagine—a financially unsuccessful morning.

Perhaps this was a one-time event. Maybe some employees failed to report for their opening shift. Possibly, but I doubt it.

If it was a one-time event I think there would be a hustle of activity in the restaurant and cars would have been lined up expecting service. The fact that there were no cars outside and no cars in the drive through, not even a sign on the door saying, "Please be patient while we get ready to serve you!" indicates that local customers are trained to expect poor service during the morning rush.

I understand that it's poor business to prepare more food than your projections show you'll sell during a shift. But I also know that when you expect to have poor results, you will. And sometimes you have to take a leap of faith, expect big results and play to win!

So what do you think would happen if that restaurant started to expect business in the morning? What if they made sure they prepared a little more food than they expected to sell? What if they started to show their customers that going there was a good choice by having the customer service we expect from a major player in the fast food industry?

Do you think they'd start to get more business if they prepared for success?

I do!

Take a moment and ask yourself, "Is there anything I can do to prepare for success?"

Well...Is there?

Perfection

We've all heard this saying about Perfection:

Practice makes perfect...

You may have also heard this twist:

Perfect practice makes perfect.

Or this one:

Imperfect practice makes perfect.

Now, all of these mean the same thing. That to improve at anything, you must work at it. But they each focus on different aspects.

The first is the simplest and is true. To improve at anything you must do it.

The second is also true. But the person who said it was emphasizing the fact that you must strive for perfection as you practice; to perfect what you are practicing...

And, like the two previous, the third is also true. But this time the emphasis is that you shouldn't expect yourself to be perfect while practicing something. You must accept your imperfections as you perfect yourself.

Which is the most relevant to you and your Life?

Think about it.

Part 1: Transformations

Is the Law of Attraction Broken?

Some people say the *Law of Attraction doesn't work, or that it's broken. (*Whatever you give your time, energy, and focus to you attract into your life.)

Case in point, I received an email a few days ago with the title, "Busted! Why the Law of Attraction Doesn't Work..."

The first thing I thought was, "What rubbish! Of course the Law of Attraction works!"

Then it popped into my mind, "But only as hard as you do."

You realize that many people spend time focusing on what they desire. But then they sit back and expect it to happen without doing anything to get it.

If that was how it worked anyone who has tried to manifest using the Law of Attraction would have everything they wanted.

But that's not how it works. You have to do something, take action, move in the direction of what you desire. You can sit in the lotus posture all day long while focusing positive thoughts and emotions on the things you desire. And you'll end up disappointed.

Or you can take the time to figure out what you desire, get clear on it subconsciously, focus on it with powerful positive emotions, AND *Move Your Feet! Take Inspired Action!*

That's when miracles happen! That's when your dreams and desires come true!

Another Slice of Pi

So stop with the excuses already. The Law of Attraction works. Use it. And then take regular action in the direction of your dream and watch the magic unfurl.

Part 1: Transformations

Get Back on The Horse.

When Life Bucks You Off, Get Back on The Horse!

What do I mean? Imagine this:

You're cruising through your day and something unexpected happens.

Wham!

What do you do?

Do you take it in stride?

Do you get sidetracked but find your way back on track?

Do you melt down?

Only you know the answer to this. But I suggest you "Get back on the horse."

So, what does that mean?

Old time cowboys relied on their horses for almost everything. They were with them in every season, through different terrain, and almost every type of weather. In many ways the horse was not only an extension of the cowboy; it was the cowboy's lifeline.

But even the best cowboy got knocked off his horse sometimes.

What do you think happened then? Do you think the cowboy sat on the ground and cried or screamed about how unfair it was that he got knocked down?

Do you think he called it a day and went home?

Not on your life! He stood up, brushed himself off, and *got back on his horse.*

Another Slice of Pi

I suggest we follow this example in our lives. There will be days when things happen that interfere with your goals. When you have a day like that, just imagine you're that old cowboy. Then pick yourself up, brush yourself up, and...

Get Back on The Horse.

Part 1: Transformations

I Don't Wanna…

Do you ever find yourself thinking this about something you know is good for you? Have you woken up early to exercise, meditate, or write and thought, "I'll just sleep for a few more minutes."?

But what happens to those few minutes?

If you're like me—and most people—those few minutes turn into an hour or so. Then the next day it's easier to "sleep in" for a few minutes. Until, in a short period of time, you've set a new habit of sleeping in.

Why does that happen?

Here are some reasons:

1. Humans like easy. And sleeping in is easy. Avoiding the resistance that accompanies growth is easy. But you know that easy rarely produces success.
2. Listening to the little voice that says, "I don't wanna…" gives it power. Like a child throwing a temper tantrum, it realizes you're paying attention and screams louder each time.

3. Habits are easier to create than most people realize. Even a slight change in your routine makes a difference. And it doesn't matter which direction your routine changes. Your brain notices you've made a change. It watches what you do the next time too. Then it tallies what you show it is important and "helps" you get more of those results.

But these things can work in your favor too.

1. When you find your true passion doing things that keep you on the path of success are far easier.
2. Just as listening to the "I don't wanna..." voice gives it power, redirecting your thoughts and doing whatever you must do instead, quiets the voice and lessens its influence.
3. A habit that carries you on the road of success is just as easy to create as a habit that sends you to the ditch. Pick something small that you know is aligned with your dream and do it regularly. In no time you'll have a habit that works for you instead of against you.

So the next time that little voice tries to talk you out of doing something that you know creates success in your life, you can say, "Thanks, but I'm doing it anyway."

Part 1: Transformations

Success and Sabotage

Which one do you feed?

I'm sure you've seen a cartoon with the little angel on one shoulder and a small devil on the other. These usually show a person's conscious and their dark side. But I think they also represent Success and Sabotage.

Success wants you to be happy. Success wants you to achieve your goals. And most important, Success believes in you.

Sabotage wants you to be miserable. Sabotage wants you to quit. And Sabotage thinks you can't do it.

When you're tired and you think maybe you should skip today's workout, that's Sabotage whispering in your ear.

When you think results aren't coming fast enough and maybe it isn't worth the effort...Yup, Sabotage.

When you're tired and you don't feel like exercising, but you do it because you promised yourself you would, that's Success.

When you're at 50 reps, you fight past the urge to stop and hit your goal, that's Success kicking Sabotage off your shoulder!

Every time you work out, every time you reach your daily goal, every time you do something that makes you a better person, it feeds Success.

Another Slice of Pi

Every time you decide to stop short of your goals, every time you skip a workout or break a promise to yourself—or others—you feed Sabotage.

The one you feed is the one that rules your life.

Who do you want running the show?

I choose Success!

Part 1: Transformations

Digging My Way to China!

When I was six I got it in my head one day that I should dig my way to China. So I grabbed my grandma's shovel and attacked her back yard.

I started with huge shovels full of dirt, the kind that spill all over—no matter how carefully you move them. But that was Hard Work! I had to jump on the shovel to get it in deep enough. Then I had to pry it up. And each one felt like it weighed a ton!

In a few minutes I started to wear down.

There was no way I was digging to China at that pace… So I stopped and leaned on my shovel. I was discouraged. Then in a flash of childhood inspiration I decided to take small bites with the shovel instead.

Curious if that would work, I renewed my quest.

I developed a rhythm without thinking. I used small steady strokes, like a metronome. I was at it for hours. In fact, the only reason I stopped was because my mom discovered what I was up to.

Let's just say she didn't share my enthusiasm for digging up my grandma's back yard!

But she was amazed at the size of the hole. :) Allowing for childhood exaggeration, it was about three feet deep and three wide. I know it came to my shoulders. That's a big hole when you're six years old.

Another Slice of Pi

What would have happened if I'd insisted on taking the biggest shovel full I could every time?

Yeah, I wouldn't have made much of a dent because I'd have given up when it got too hard.

But isn't that how life is?

We seem to think we have to take the biggest step we can, every time!

Does that make sense?

Imagine if the people in your city used exaggerated movement for everything they did. Sober people would serve all over the road. Power walkers would do the splits with every step. Shaking hands would be an exercise in combat skill.

So why should every step you take toward your dream be the biggest, baddest step you can take? That gets overwhelming. It leads toward sporadic progress and can be the death of a dream.

Why not take meaningful, manageable, consistent steps instead? Why not do something—even something small—every day that is in the direction of your dream?

The magic of small steps is this: They Add Up!

Yeah, maybe I didn't make it to China. But I accomplished a lot more that day than I would have if I'd quit because of overwhelm.

Start today. Think of something that moves you toward your dreams. And Do It!

Part 1: Transformations

A Unique Approach

It seems like many self-help programs are designed around getting things.

You set goals to get things. You improve yourself, your sales skills, your…whatever, to get more stuff.

It's great to have or get stuff. Let me make that clear. Money is neutral. It is a wonderful tool if you choose to make it one.

My book, *Your Blueprint, Life by Design*, is different. I take a unique approach. And though "getting more stuff" certainly happens when you follow the guidelines and aim yourself that direction, the book is really about learning to be the ideal you. It's about learning how to be the miracle you want to be in the world.

Once you figure that out the rest begins to fall into place.

It was a little over two years ago that I had the thought that gave birth to "Your Blueprint, Life by Design".

I'd learned a lot about the Law of Attraction and was using it to attract some "stuff" in my life. I was also making changes in my personal life and my thought processes. Some people told me I was stuck, that I'd never make those changes while some people were supportive. But I knew it was up to me. Like Atlas, the world of change was on my shoulders.

I was scared. "Could I do it?" I often wondered.

And then it hit me, "What if I use the Law of Attraction to attract the ideal me?"

Another Slice of Pi

That's when I started using everything I knew about the Law of Attraction and Subconscious Mind Power to recreate myself. That's when I discovered that designing my life as a whole allowed the smaller bits to come together.

And you know what?

I made changes I was told were impossible!

And that's where "Your Blueprint, Life by Design" came from. It's designed to empower you to recreate your life, to change yourself from the inside out. Heck, to rebuild your entire life if you must.

You are more powerful than you probably imagine! You are a miracle! You are an amazing and capable person! Maybe that scares you. Maybe it excites you. Either way, I'm honored you've chosen me as one of your guides.

Part 1: Transformations

Are You Listening?

Today I had an appointment to install a new firewall.

I got to the office early, double checked that I had everything I needed for the install and started to drive away. But then I had a feeling, "Look in the firewall's box."

Now this was a new firewall. Everything should be in the box. But I shrugged, pulled back into my parking spot, opened my trunk, and looked inside the box...

There was supposed to be a two part power supply. Half was missing.

That would have been a problem because this client is over two hours away.

Thankfully I've trained myself to listen to my gut, to those hunches I get. And because I listened, my delay was minimal. I tracked down the other half of the power supply and got on the road.

This might seem like a small thing. And in the grand scheme of life it is. But there are times when listening to your hunches can be the difference between success and disaster, even life and death.

And the key is this. If you learn to listen and trust those feelings, you'll notice them more and more.

They will guide you. And I've personally never been led astray when I was listening.

So open your ears, and your heart. Pay attention to the voice inside. Discover the difference this one thing can make in your life...if you let it.

Another Slice of Pi

What is The Cost of A Smile?

Does a smile cost you anything? Do you smile easily? Or, do you walk around with a serious expression, maybe even a frown?

What impact do you think your facial expression has on others?

Take that a step further. Ask yourself, "What impact do my facial expressions have on me?"

Check yourself right now. Are you smiling?

If so, great! How do you feel?

If not, why not? And again, how do you feel?

Try something for me. Stop right now. Get up and go stand in front of a mirror. Put a big, genuine smile on your face. Now smile at yourself in the mirror for 30 to 60 seconds. Make eye contact with yourself. Feel happy and confident. After all, you do like yourself.

Yeah, yeah, people might think you're weird.

SO WHAT!

I know an author isn't supposed to tell people to stop reading. But this is important. Besides, I know you'll come back and finish.

So, go now! Smile at yourself in the mirror for 30 to 60 seconds and then come back and tell me how you feel.

Deal?

.

.

.

Part 1: Transformations

.
.
.
.
.
.
.
.
.

Did I wait long enough?

Good.

How do you feel now?

Great! I knew you'd feel better. Even if you felt good or great to start, it's impossible to smile at yourself with a genuine, warm smile and not feel better.

Why is that?

It's because your brain is hardwired to react positively to a smile. A smile is an open, friendly, accepting gesture. It sends a message of welcome and love. That makes smiles infectious! I think you'll agree with me, of all the diseases in this world I can't think of one I'd rather have than chronic Smileyitis.

Now imagine what your smile does for the people you interact with every day...

I know when I smile, which is all the time, I see many happy, friendly people smiling back at me. My smile feeds their smile and their smile feeds my smile. It's a wonderful loop of positive reinforcement!

In fact, total strangers approach me all the time. They smile, I smile, and we have pleasant conversations. It's wonderful.

But it wasn't always that way. I used to walk around with a grim set to my mouth. I frowned a lot and didn't realize it. In effect I wore a huge, "Leave me alone!" sign. And you know what, even though that wasn't what I thought I wanted, it worked.

People avoided me like the plague.

That's not what I wanted. But that's reality. When you walk around with a dark cloud hanging over you, others see it. And they feel it. When you choose to be miserable, you impact those around you. Even if you try to keep it to yourself, they will sense it and it will affect them.

Is that what you want?

Or...do you want to lift the spirits of the people you meet every day?

With that in mind, ask yourself, "What is the cost of a smile?"

My answer is this: A smile costs nothing. It's an investment in the beauty of life!

Part 1: Transformations

How Do You Approach Life?

Have you ever noticed that some people approach life like a sprint? They run hard and fast and then keel over from exhaustion. After lying there awhile they might get back up and sprint some more. But often they'll flounder for a long time before mustering the courage for the next sprint. They do make progress of sorts, but it's sporadic.

Then there are people who walk slowly through life. They never really get started. They never accomplish much. But they do keep moving—albeit slowly.

You might think the middle ground is the person who approached life like a marathon runner. And there are good qualities about that philosophy. The steady motion is faster than walking.

But what about when sprinting is the only way to achieve your goal?

Some marathoners are up to it and some aren't. Many walkers will shrug and think, "Oh well...not today."

That where intervals come in. An interval is when you sprint for a set distance and then run or walk for a while and then sprint again. When you approach life with an interval mentality you're willing to adjust your speed to fit the situation.

That's how I approach life. My life isn't a slow leisurely stroll and it isn't a long marathon. It is one amazing Interval session.

Another Slice of Pi

I challenge you to do the same!

Face it. Sometimes you have to sprint! Sometimes jogging or walking is wise. But when you're flexible in your approach, you can keep moving no matter what happens.

Part 1: Transformations

Letting Go of "Why?"

I had an awakening the other night. I realized I was holding onto "Why?" about some things that happened to me as a child. I realized this after a memory was triggered that left me on the floor emotionally.

I sat there thinking, "Why did that happen to me?"

When one of my friends asked me what was wrong, I actually said, "I can't talk about it."

Now if you know me, you know that "Can't" goes against everything I believe in.

A few minutes later I shook my head, looked at my friend, and said, "You know I hate the word 'Can't'. I'm not going to let myself get away with that...." Then I talked about what was bothering me.

That was a step in the right direction. It aligns with who I am instead of who I used to be. But I still felt emotionally raw for the rest of the night. And, truth be told, I felt sorry for myself.

I know feeling sorry for myself accomplishes nothing. So I worked to get out of that state. I thought about the good that came from those things in my childhood. I thought about how grateful I am for everything in my life. Those methods usually improve my mood quickly.

Yet every time I was still—not actively doing something to lift my mood—I felt the sadness squeeze back in.

Another Slice of Pi

So I set the bloodhounds of introspection loose in my mind.

They came back with interesting news.

"Everyone in here is still wondering why those things happened to you." The lead hound said. Proud that he'd solved the riddle.

I thought on that. And it was true. In the quiet spaces of my mind I was still wondering "Why?".

I'd refused to let myself get away with "Can't" but was busy staring in the rearview mirror.

That's when I sat down and had a nice talk with myself.

"You know those things are fixed, immovable." I said.

"I know..." I answered

"And you know you'll most likely never know the answer to why they happened." I said.

"Yeah," I sniffed.

"So let it go. Let go of 'Why?'." I encouraged myself.

"Ok." I said.

Giving myself permission to let go of "Why?" started a healing process. Over the next 24 hours I regained my footing and the quiet spaces in my mind returned to optimism, joy, and hope. Simply put, making the conscious decision to let go of "Why?" allowed me to move on.

Does this mean I'll never have a moment when I feel that way again?

Maybe, maybe not. But it means I know how to handle it when it happens.

What about you?

Is there a "Why?" you're holding onto?

If there is, please be gentle on yourself. Realize that holding onto that "Why?" must have served a purpose in the past.

Part 1: Transformations

And know that it's ok to release it now and to move on with your life. After all, now it's holding you back.

Good luck and God Bless.

Another Slice of Pi

Accountability and Happiness

Listen to the world around you. You're sure to hear excuses about almost everything.

"I was late because my car broke down."

"I'm broke because I'm stuck in a low paying job."

"I'm unhappy because I don't make enough money."

"I'm unhappy because I don't have the things I want."

And on and on...

Few people are willing to say:

"I was late because I didn't take care of my car."

"I'm in a low paying job because I refuse to get training."

Or...

"I'm unhappy because I choose to be."

So, is it any coincidence that few people are truly happy? Hmmm... Maybe there's a relationship between accountability and happiness.

What do you think?

Do you think people who accept complete accountability for their lives make excuses as a matter of course?

I don't think so.

But what is it about accepting total accountability that breeds happiness? After all, some people might look at accepting accountability as a way to increase their guilt—then they can blame themselves for everything.

Well, I've got news for you. If a person is "blaming themselves" for everything, they aren't accepting accountability.

Part 1: Transformations

They're choosing to be the victim of circumstance. That's different from accountability.

To be accountable for your life means to take responsibility for your thoughts, your actions, the state of your life, and the impact your actions have on others.

How is that different from taking the blame?

Simple.

When a person takes blame, they are closed to the fact that they can choose to change. They look at undesirable results in their life as punishment instead of lessons for improvement. They look for reasons to feel bad. A person who looks for reasons to feel bad is in a cycle of negative-reinforcement.

Is that a proactive or empowering place to be?

So, what is it about accepting total accountability that creates happiness?

Here's the secret: People who accept total accountability for their lives know that if they don't like the results they're getting, they can change their thoughts and actions and get different results!

They experience the freedom of creating their destiny.

Knowing that you create your destiny, that you can change your results and your life... That's a powerful and happy place to live.

How do you accept accountability and take control of your life?

Start by listening to yourself.

What words do you use? Do you say: Can't, Couldn't, or But?

When you talk about something that happened—good or bad—do you focus on the things that caused it?

Another Slice of Pi

If you do, you might feel like the victim of circumstance. If you feel like a victim of circumstance it's challenging to accept accountability.

Combat this and create awareness now. Realize what you say. Listen to yourself. Take your mind—and mouth—off autopilot. Choose empowering phrases like, "I did" or "I can" or "I am". When you talk about things that happened to you, look for results that your choices produced.

Maybe, "I didn't have time to write that report." becomes, "I chose to watch a movie instead of writing that report." Or, "I lucked out and passed the test." becomes, "even though I didn't study as much as I should have, I passed the test because I paid attention in class."

Then, as you accept more accountability, you begin to realize the amazing power you have over the results you get from life. After all, accountability means accepting credit for things you do right too!

Part 1: Transformations

Fear; Is It In You?

Fear... Do you feel it?

It's there when you do something new the first time. When you play bigger than yourself and surpass your wildest expectations, it's there—at least in the beginning. Then you get lost in the moment, in the flow, and fear disappears.

But what happens when you choose to listen to fear? What happens when you let it convince you that you really shouldn't try?

"What if you fail?" it asks like a concerned friend. And then reasons, "Isn't it better to just leave it alone than to fail?"

Ask yourself this, "What if I succeed?"

Can you ever succeed if you quit? Sure you might fail a few times while you're getting the hang of something. But you fail permanently when you quit.

What do you do when the voice of fear enters your mind? And let's be clear, I'm talking about the fear of doing things that stretch your comfort zone. If you're standing on train tracks and hear a whistle and feel the tracks shaking, you'd better listen to that fear and get off the tracks. But if you're sitting in your chair and you're afraid to join the discussion, or you're standing on the edge of the dance floor afraid to ask someone to dance, or you're staying home from the gym because you're afraid what people will think about you... Those voices of fear might have power but the truth is none of those things can hurt you if you do them.

Another Slice of Pi

The way I feel about it is that fear—unless it's of imminent physical harm—is a sign that I'd better get out there and do the thing that frightens me.

Writing the first post for this blog was scary. Writing my book," Your Blueprint, Life by Design" was scary. Where would I be if I'd listened to those fears? And most important to me, where would you be if I'd listened to those fears.

Courage is taking action in the face of fear. It matters little what you fear, it matters a lot that you find your courage and do the thing that frightens you. Even if it's a little step, it chips away at fear. Soon you'll laugh that you were ever afraid of that!

I challenge you to look for things—again healthy things :)—that you fear. And start doing them.

You'll be amazed how fast you grow and how quickly the fear disappears!

Part 1: Transformations

Phoenix

Have you ever had one of those moments when it seemed life flash-burned around you?

One minute everything was great and the next, POOF! A giant fireball leaves you standing in the ashes of your dreams.

Or maybe everything wasn't so great. Maybe it felt like you were barely holding the threads of your life together... Then they snapped and everything exploded around you.

I don't know if you've experienced that moment. I don't know what the situation was if you have. I know what it felt like when I had that moment though. And I know this; at that moment you have a powerful choice to make. You can choose to be the victim or you can choose to *be the Phoenix* and rise from the ashes like a miracle. More beautiful, more capable, more powerful than you ever were before.

What if you created the situation that flashed burned your life? Does that mean the Phoenix isn't in you?

Sorry, you're not off the hook that easy.

You're human. You have a brain. You are capable of learning and making better choices. Ergo, you can choose to be different, to figure out what went wrong and learn how to avoid those mistakes in the future.

That means you can choose to *unlock your Phoenix*.

And it doesn't matter if your napalm moment happened yesterday or ten years ago, you can release your Phoenix and

Another Slice of Pi

start rising today. It's never too late to change. It's never too late to be the miracle in your life and the lives of others.

A great place to start this journey is to ask yourself these questions:

1. "What good is in this situation?" (What good came from it or can come from it?)
2. "What lessons are in this situation for me?"
3. "How can I use this to become a better person?"

And my favorite question, "How can I use this to benefit others?" How can you use the knowledge you've gained to be the miracle in the life of another?

Those can be hard questions. But I promise you this; when you start asking them, you'll discover the ashes aren't as thick as you thought. Then you'll begin to rise from the ruins as the beautiful, capable, powerful Phoenix that you've always been.

Part 1: Transformations

Impressionable

How Impressionable Are We?

The other day my three year old daughter, Bethany, was playing intently with her dolls. She held them close to each other and moved them around while bobbing her head and talking softly.

Curious about the conversation her dolls were having, I moved closer.

"No," She said in a sweet voice and moved the doll that was talking, "I'm locked in my room by my wicked step-mother. I can't come out to play."

That floored me.

I thought about how impressionable children are. My daughter doesn't have a step-parent. She has no reference point to make that comment.

Or Does she?

I'm sure you've seen Sleeping Beauty or Cinderella. Well, my innocent daughter has watched them both a number of times. They are some of her favorite shows. They are rated G after all!

So isn't it amazing that she picked up the concept of a "Wicked Step-Mother" and that to her it's just a matter of course? I know she doesn't understand what wicked is. But in her mind that phrase is waiting for the day she's old enough to comprehend it. (Thankfully, now that I know that belief is there, I can help her change it.)

Another Slice of Pi

That's how many of our beliefs are formed though. We hear and see things when we're young and our subconscious mind accepts them as "The way it is".

You might be surprised to learn that your subconscious mind does that your entire life.

Have heart though. You can retrain your brain. You can change your subconscious beliefs. And when you do, you change your life!

If you want a proven system that shows you how to re-program your subconscious mind and recreate your life, just hop over to http://www.rolandbyrd.co/books-by-roland-byrd/your-blueprint-life-by-design/ and grab your copy of *"Your Blueprint, Life by Design"* today!

Part 1: Transformations

Do It Anyway.

I saw this quote in a client's office a few days ago. It is beautiful and enlightened and I felt I must share it with you.

"People are often unreasonable and self-centered. Forgive them anyway.

"If you are kind, people may accuse you of ulterior motives. Be kind anyway.

"If you are honest, people may cheat you. Be honest anyway.

"If you find happiness, people may be jealous. Be happy anyway.

"The good you do today may be forgotten tomorrow. Do good anyway.

"Give the world the best you have and it may never be enough. Give your best anyway.

"For you see, in the end, it is between you and God. It was never between you and them anyway." — Mother Teresa

Remember

You Are the Master of Your Destiny!

Detached Intention Part 1

You want something. You set goals, review those goals, and are super positive about it. But it isn't happening!

What's going wrong?

It could be a number of things. But let's focus on a Key Factor to manifesting what you want: Detached Intention.

The reason you aren't manifesting your desire could be how badly you *think* you need it. I didn't say how badly you want it. You can want something more than anything without feeling like you need it.

What's the difference?

When you want something, you realize life will go on without it. But it *would* be nice to have.

When you need something, especially when you need (or think you need) it badly, it's easy to worry about whether or not you get it. But worrying about the outcome is a sure fire way to guarantee you don't get what you want!

I'll use sales people for this example. I can do that because I've done plenty of sales in my time. ;-) But this scenario applies to any situation where you *needed* something and it didn't happen.

Have you ever thought you had a sale wrapped up? But you *needed* the money... So you dwelled on your need for money and thoughts of doubt snuck into your mind? Then you played with the doubts, like you'd play with a loose tooth, didn't you?

Part 1: Transformations

What happened?

Most likely the sale fell through the cracks. The prospect disappeared or they came up with a reason they didn't need your product. Or something else happened. But ultimately the sale disintegrated.

What did you say to yourself then?

Was something like, "I knew it wasn't going to work out!" Or, "I had a feeling something bad was going to happen."

Well, guess what?

Those feelings of doubt and worry were part of the sale falling apart!

Why?

Because those feelings created negative emotions and vibrations, which repelled the very thing you *needed*.

Remember, the Law of Attraction doesn't care why you're radiating negative vibrations, it just acknowledges that you are and gives you more of the same. When vibrations of worry and doubt blast from you like heat from a bonfire, the Law of Attraction obliges you and withdraws *the thing you need*—because you aren't in harmony with it.

Please understand; it's ok to need things. We all know there are many things in life that are more than wants. Food is a need. Water is a need. Love and connection with other human beings are needs. It's alright to need things. Just realize that needs and wants—cloaked as needs—are different creatures.

And it doesn't matter if something is a want or a need, worry and doubt *still* repel it.

I'm not sure who said this, "*Worry is a prayer for something negative to happen.*" But it makes the point beautifully.

Another Slice of Pi

When you worry about something you give it loads of attention, which because you're focused on an undesired outcome, creates negative energy. As you know, this draws the undesired outcome to you because giving *Time Energy and Focus* is a how you manifest something.

With that in mind, ask yourself, "Am I *attracting* undesirable things or *desirable* things?"

If you're not sure which it is, just pay attention to your persistent thoughts. Do you think about what you want to happen or what you don't want to happen? Your thoughts are your focus.

And the outcome you focus on *is the one you attract*.

So if you're worried about something bad happening, how do you focus on a positive outcome?

You don't.

That's where the power of *Detached Intention* comes in. Detached Intention means you intend for the outcome you want to happen, but you're detached emotionally from how, when, or whether it comes to pass.

Does being detached emotionally from the outcome mean you aren't excited about it?

Hardly! It just means you let go of concerns and negative feelings about "not getting" your desired outcome. It means you *Stop Worrying* about what might happen and you *let it happen*.

When you *stop worrying*, your mind is free from chains of negativity and open to feelings of abundance, gratitude, and expectation. These are natural feelings that *should* accompany your desires; they also help you manifest your desires as quickly as possible.

Part 1: Transformations

Stay tuned. In Monday's post, I'll reveal a few proven ways to *stop worrying* and *focus on what you want* instead of what you don't.

Detached Intention Part 2

You worry when you focus on what you don't want to happen or what you're afraid will happen. Ironically your worry attracts what you're worried about.

So, how do you stop worrying?

Change your focus.

If you want to stop worry in its tracks then replace thoughts of worry with thoughts of success. Train yourself to do this automatically. When you notice you're worrying, immediately ask yourself, "What outcome do I want?" Then start thinking about that outcome!

Go ahead, daydream about your successful outcome. This replaces worry because you can't worry about something while you're envisioning your successful outcome.

Make this a habit and you'll soon find that thoughts of worry cancel themselves. Then, when you notice worry creeping in, your brain automatically shifts to thoughts of success!

It's like Pavlov's dog. The dog sees and smells food and hears a bell. This is repeated over and over until the dog salivates when it hears a bell! No food required.

Your brain reacts the same way. Replace thoughts of worry with thoughts of success enough times and it hardwires your brain. Then worry becomes the bell that produces thoughts of success!

Give this a shot for a few weeks and let me know how it works for you!

Part 1: Transformations

What Are the Odds?

Do You Realize How Miraculous You Are?

What are the odds that you would be born in this world at this time in history? What are the odds that all the events in your life unfolded in the perfect orchestration which helped you become you?

I've no idea. But I know they're astronomical.

Now whether you're religious or not, you must realize this: The fact that you are you is amazing.

You are a miracle! So Be The Miracle!

Any time you think less of yourself or are tempted to speak ill of yourself, please remember how wondrous you are. You have the power to be whoever you want. You have the power to choose happiness in your life. You have gifts and talents that are unique and valuable. You are a perfect creation of God, a perfect manifestation of you!

If you aren't happy with your life or with who you've chosen to be, then change.

Make the decision today. Dare to be better, to play bigger, to live up to your dreams. Dare to be the miracle in your life and the lives of others.

Seriously... What have you got to lose?

Another Slice of Pi

Easter and Forgiveness

For me Easter is a time to reflect on the beauty of life. It's a celebration of human kind's ability to rise above imperfection, to shed past mistakes and begin anew. And most of all, it is a time to reflect on the beauty of forgiveness.

I usually stay away from discussions on religion. But today I must thank God, my creator, for the gifts I've been given, for the power of the atonement that allows me to come back from sin and to find renewed hope and purpose in my life. Everything I am and everything I do is possible because of my creator.

Today is the perfect celebration of that.

I hope that no matter your religious beliefs, you understand the power forgiveness. Forgiveness heals the wounded heart. It releases you from the chains of hate. It acknowledges the past and creates a future of hope and beauty.

Forgiveness is a miracle cure.

So today I challenge you to take a moment and look in your heart. Is there something you're holding onto? It doesn't matter if it's small or something life-altering, when you choose to forgive you release yourself from the power it has over you. The shift might be slow or it might happen in a second. But your life will change when you choose to forgive.

Happy Easter and God Bless!

Part 1: Transformations

The Beauty of Now

Do You Ever Feel Like You're Rushing Through Life?

It's easy to get caught in the pattern that "you have to get somewhere now", to race through life seeking destination after destination, goal after goal. But then you end up looking back and wondering where yesterday went. You might stand atop the summit of your life with little memory of the events that brought you there. Your life ends up a blur. Then what do you have to show for it?

I submit this for your consideration.

Life *is* the Destination.

Make sure you appreciate The Beauty of Now, the Miracles that are happening around you this very moment!

Look around. See the wonderful people in your life. See the beauty of your surroundings. Notice the colors and the patterns that enfold you.

Listen to your life. Hear the unique sounds of your life. What are the tempos? Is there laughter, rainfall, chaos? Everything you hear is unique to you because no one else hears exactly the same way you do.

Feel your life. Pay attention to your life's sensations. What emotions do you experience? What tactile impressions happen in your day? What does it feel like to walk or run or sit or exercise or play? What does it feel like to hold the hand of someone you love?

Taste your life. You eat things all the time. What are the flavors that most appeal to you? What happens with your mouth every day? As a child you explored the world by putting things in your mouth. While I hardly recommend that approach as an adult, you can still realize the wonderful flavors of your life.

All these things work together to help you appreciate the power and beauty of now.

A destination is of little consequence when the journey is wasted. Do you really want your life to be like the commute where you get in your car and then blink because you've arrived?

So pay attention to your life. Pay attention to the people in it and the things that happen every day. Start seeing the beauty in every moment, every perfect moment that creates you.

Understand; goals are good. Knowing where you're going is key to creating success. Just make sure you enjoy life while you're seeking your dreams. You never know the magic that will happen today if you just open yourself to experiencing it.

Part 1: Transformations

Tear it Down!

Sometimes You Have to Tear it Down and Rebuild.

The Dojo where I train is undergoing a major renovation. Last night I helped clean rubble from the demolition phase of the project.

They'd ripped out the old interior walls and flooring. That left a pile of debris about 30 feet wide and 6 feet tall right in the middle of the floor.

What a mess!

It felt daunting, the idea of cleaning up that massive pile of plaster, wood, and metal. But I started anyway. One piece a time, one shovel full after another, I threw the innards of the old Dojo in the dumpster.

And something cool happened. I entered a peaceful and meditative state. Before I knew it, half the pile was gone and the vision of the new Dojo was firmly planted in my mind.

That got me thinking about life. Sometimes we have to remodel, to tear down the old and rebuild when we desire something better. This is scary for most people. After all, you spent your whole life getting where you are today.

But ask yourself these questions:

"Is where I am today working for me?"

"Is my life what I imagined it would be?"

"Is it possible to make my life better?"

Those answers tell you if you need to remodel.

Another Slice of Pi

Now you might need a complete demo and rebuild. The kind where you get away from the old friends and situations and habits that help you justify staying in a flawed or unhealthy lifestyle—and if you do there are many organizations that will help you through this process.

Or you might just need to tear the carpet out of a single room of your life and lay something better.

Either way there are two things to remember.

1. There are resources to help you.

2. Today is the best day to start. When you wait until tomorrow, tomorrow becomes an elusive creature that seems forever out of reach.

If you are in need of a major overhaul, please seek assistance. This can come from a counselor, a group like AAA or Al-Anon, or other places. And if you're not sure where to go for help then look to your local church. Many times they have information about community resources that are designed to assist you.

The key is to take action now. Do something today that creates the change in your life. Before you know it you'll have a firm vision of the new tomorrow in your mind. In time you'll look back and wonder why you ever feared the change.

Part 1: Transformations

The Secret to Life

Do You Know The Secret to Life?

The other day I jokingly asked my seven year old son if he wanted to know the secret to life.

Well...he bit.

"Dad," he asked, "What is it?"

I wasn't prepared for the question—which was silly since I'd asked him that. But after thinking a moment I said, "The secret to life is that you can choose happiness."

But it's simpler than that. The real secret is that you can choose. You—and everyone else on this planet myself included—have the power of choice.

We weren't given the power to control everything that happens in our lives. But we were given the power to choose how we react or respond to everything that happens to us.

What an amazing gift!

That means if you want a happy life, choose it. If you want a successful life, make the choices that create it. If you want emotional, physical, mental, and spiritual health; then start making choices that bring you that direction.

Now maybe you're thinking, "Easy for you to say...but my life really bites right now!"

Well, if that's the case then I'm sorry that things are rough. I really am.

I can promise you this though, if you look for it, there is something in your life worth celebrating at this very mo-

Another Slice of Pi

ment. Perhaps it's the sun shining on your face or the sound of a nearby bird or even the shape of that dark cloud on the horizon. Maybe it's as simple as the fact that you have some clothes to wear or a roof over your head or even a park bench to sleep on or a car to sleep in.

I have no idea what your situation is. But I know there are miracles in your life and if you choose to look you'll find something to choose happiness about. And then you'll discover that the more you choose happiness, the easier it is to find reason to feel happy!

Go ahead and give it a shot! What have you got to lose?

If you're making those choices already, then kudos to you!

Part 1: Transformations

Michelangelo's David

Have you ever seen the statue David by Michelangelo?

How do you think he made it? Did he smash a sledge hammer against that block of marble and reveal David in one stroke?

Hardly!

He used multiple tools. He slowly chipped away at the imperfections and polished the marble. When he finished the statue David remained. It's a masterpiece that stands the test of time.

Do you think we'd celebrate his work if he'd taken the first approach?

What about your life? Think about the things you want to accomplish. Are you taking the single hit with a sledge hammer approach, or the Michelangelo approach?

When Michelangelo first set the chisel to that block of marble he knew it was going to take consistent, effort. I imagine he knew it was going to take time to reveal the statue within. And that he knew his efforts would only succeed if he showed up every day and did something.

I encourage you to show up every day to your life. Whatever you're trying to accomplish, a small step every day will help you be the Miracle in your life and the life of other's. They add up and you'll notice Amazing results in no time.

Where Are You Going?

Where are you going with your life?

Have you planned how to get there?

Are you purposefully engaged in doing something that matters to you or do you float along like a wind tossed leaf, jumping and spinning from one thing to the next?

I'll let you in on a secret. Unless you know your destination, or at least its general vicinity, you'll never reach it.

How can you?

But once you figure out what you're passionate about and you know where you're going, that's when magic happens. Add persistent action to the mix and...

Watch out World!

I know what it's like to dream of something better but have no idea what it was or how to get there. But then I learned the importance of discovering my passion. That helped my know where I was going and why I wanted to get there.

That's when my life changed.

I want to offer you the same gift. So I'm making my "*Discover Your Passion*" report available to anyone who wants it.

Just click here to Discover Your Passion:

http://www.rolandbyrd.co/ynbp/bookbonuses/Discover%20Your%20Passion.pdf

Part 1: Transformations

It's in Your Mind!

Did you know that Everything You Do starts in your mind?

The thought comes first, then the action. The thought might be subconscious, but it's there.

That might feel discouraging to some. If everything you do starts with a thought in your mind...

Yeah, it means accountability. Many people shy away from that concept. But I think the great thing about this knowledge is that it gives you the power to take control of your life.

How?

Simple. You can choose your thoughts.

Now you might say, "I have little control over the thoughts I have."

Really?

You might not always have direct control over what thoughts spring into your mind. But you always have control over what you do with those thoughts. You also have control over what you're filling your head with.

Consider this: Many of your thoughts result from the programming your subconscious mind receives every day.

What are you filling your head with? What do you listen to, watch, read? What's the topic of conversation at work or with friends?

Those all contribute to who you are and how you think.

Another Slice of Pi

It boils down this. If you don't like the output, then change the input!

You'll notice a big difference in time.

If you want proven methods to change your input and your life, Read "Your Blueprint, Life by Design" and "Break Your Mold: The Art of Overcoming Patterns and Behaviors That Hold You Back".

You'll find them both here:

http://www.rolandbyrd.co/books-by-roland-byrd/

Part 1: Transformations

Be Yourself!

If there's one thing I've learned it's that I have to be myself.

I used to think being a carbon copy of someone successful would make me successful.

Nope!

It just made me an unsuccessful mimic.

When I stopped mimicking others I discovered I had something to offer and I grew into a new level of my life.

This was most apparent when I wrote "Your Blueprint, Life by Design." I found my voice and wrote by inspiration. Writing it was fun because I was being me.

Where I'm going with this is that sometimes we get caught up trying to act like someone else who's successful.

That rarely works. But it can be amusing to watch.

There's a difference between using the system another used for success and mimicking that person. Remember to be you. That's key. You're an amazing person with tremendous potential. You are a miracle in your own right. Be yourself. Be the Miracle!

After all, you were born to be you.

So be yourself!

No matter which success system you use, think of the steps as an outline. The real power of the system always comes from what you give it. And the best gift you can give yourself is to discover who you are and what you're good at. Then apply that knowledge to the success system.

Another Slice of Pi

Some people write. Some people dance. Some sing. Others figure out complex equations while some work magic with a sewing machine or table saw. The point is that no matter who you are, *you have a gift you can use on your path to success.*

If you aren't sure what your gift is then spend some time figuring it out. One way is to download my free "[Discover Your Passion](#)" report.

If you know your gift then brainstorm on ways you will use it to help others. That's the quickest path to fulfillment.

As Steve Jobs said, "Your time is limited, so don't waste it living someone else's life."

Part 1: Transformations

How do You Feel About Wealthy People?

I talked with a man awhile back who bemoaned his financial state and ranted against wealthy people at every opportunity. The gist of his opinion was this. Wealthy people didn't deserve their money and anyone with money was a bad person because honest people didn't acquire or keep wealth.

I asked him a few open ended questions about the value of money and the good people do with it. His answers showed that he was entrenched in his beliefs. His opinions about money and the people who have it went beyond beliefs and were fact in his mind.

I mentioned some very wealthy people I know who are wonderful philanthropists. I emphasized the good they did with their money...

He shot back that they were selfish because they didn't give more and that they only gave because of tax breaks.

I tactfully removed myself from conversation and left him to his opinions.

The truth is that I know many wealthy people who give and give and give. And they do it because they want to help others. That's wonderful!

That brings us back to the question, "How do you feel about wealthy people?"

Another Slice of Pi

What you may not realize is that your opinion of wealthy people directly affects your ability to make money.

If you hate wealthy people, how can you ever become wealthy? Doing so would put you in conflict with yourself. It would make you someone you hate. Your subconscious mind won't allow that.

So if you want to improve your financial situation, a good place to start is to look at your beliefs about money and the people who have it. If you discover those beliefs are holding you back, then you can start changing them by consciously celebrating wealthy people.

For example:

When you see a nice car say to yourself: "Good for you!" or "What an amazing car!"

When you see a mansion or expensive home say to yourself: "What a wonderful place to live. Good for them!"

You get the idea. Do that often enough and it will become a habit. Once it becomes a habit your subconscious mind will start developing new beliefs about money and will allow you to have more.

Part 1: Transformations

Urgent or Important

Do you ever let little things get in the way of important things?

Sometimes I do.

Earlier this year I stopped exercising. It wasn't an overnight decision. It was a process of finding small reasons to put each workout off. Before I knew it I'd gone two and a half months without exercising!

In the past—before I learned that I was 100% accountable for my life—I would have felt like a failure. That would have become a self-fulfilling prophecy and whammo! I'd still be lamenting all the things that "Got in the way" of my working out. I'd have gone into a downward spiral and I'd still be sitting here wondering why I didn't have time to exercise.

Instead I stopped and thought, "This isn't working... What can I do to make time to exercise again?" I brainstormed about it and came up with three simple answers.

1. Go to bed earlier.
2. Get up and exercise in time to start my day.
3. Start!

So I started doing those three easy things. Now I've been exercising again for two months. And it's easy because exercising is habit I've had for over six years now.

This is true of everything in life. Sometimes we let little things get in the way of important things. "Urgent" gets handled whether or not it's "Important" and "Important" things that lack the appearance of "Urgency" fall to the side.

That's called the "Crisis Mode" of management and it only works for so long because everything Important becomes Urgent when ignored long enough.

If there's something Important in your life that you've been putting off Today is the perfect day to start doing it!

The other important thing is to remember that you can choose your way out of a good habit, but you can just as easily choose your way back into it.

Part 1: Transformations

Sidetracked?

Did you ever get sidetracked in life?

Have you ever stopped and wondered, "How did I get here?" or "What happened to my life?"

Maybe your life headed south when you thought you were going north. Maybe you had a plan but things didn't work out the way you wanted and now your destination seems like the pot of gold at the end of a rainbow.

That can happen. But does it mean you should give up on your dream?

No.

When you're not living toward your dream—or don't know what your passion is—it's easy to get sidetracked. When that happens you might end up on a tangent that has nothing to do with your dream. That's when you're being tossed by the storms of life. Without purpose and passion—that comes from knowing who you are and where you're going—you drift.

But when you're living toward your dream, things happen. Opportunities present themselves that never would have if you walked a different path. These might carry you away from your original destination. But if you're aligned with your passion they bring you to something better. A perfect destination you'd never imagined.

Life presents us with opportunities every day. It's up to us to reach out and grasp them! Just as when life presents us with challenges, it's up to us to find the good in them.

Another Slice of Pi

When you learn to seize opportunities and turn challenges into stepping stones, you're on the true path of success.

You can start by opening yourself to the possibility that you are an amazing person with unique gifts.

You can also ask yourself these questions when you see a challenge before you:

"How can this help me grow?"

"What good is in this challenge?"

Remember it's up to you where your life goes. Only you can live it.

Part 1: Transformations

Memorial Day

Memorial Day is set aside to honor Men and Women who've died in military service. It's a day to reflect and give thanks for the sacrifices so many people have made during the course of America's history.

I would also like to personally thank all the men and women that currently serve—or have served—in military branches.

Some people agree with the US's Military efforts over the years. Some people disagree with them.

I'll stay out of that conversation.

I do know that people who give service to the military sacrifice much in their efforts to do what they believe best for the U.S. Voluntary service also prevents things like the Draft being reinstated. And that helps people who do not support the U.S.'s military efforts from being placed in military service—as has happened in the past.

So please, no matter your personal view on the validity of the U.S.A.'s military efforts in the past or present, take the time to reflect on the sacrifice these men and women have made. Thank them in your hearts for service rendered.

Thank you!

Got Anger?

If you have children then you've heard, "He made me do it!" or "She made me do it!"

Young children don't understand that they are in control of their actions and responses. Teaching them accountability is part of a parent's duty. And many parents do a wonderful job raising happy, healthy, children who understand these concepts.

But many people make it to adulthood with the idea that others control what happens in their lives. They say things like "You made me so mad." Or "You made me late for work."

When talking about things that happened or how they feel, their language is peppered with "You this" and "You that" or "They this" and "They that."

And the truly sad part is they believe it. They believe their life is out of their control. They believe others control their emotions.

But the truth about emotions is they're fleeting. The only time they have lasting impact is when you chooses to focus on them.

If you feel angry and continually think about what you're angry about, you're throwing fuel on your anger. It's like a bonfire. If you add fuel it grows and can easily get out of control. If you leave it alone it burns down quickly. If you put enough water on it, it goes out completely.

Part 1: Transformations

To put water on that fire just think about something you're grateful for or something you feel happy about. Anger and happiness cannot exist in the same place at the same time. Neither can anger and gratitude.

Sadly, there are people who have something unfortunate happen to them and then spend most of their lives throwing fuel on their personal bonfire. They end up with a raging forest fire of anger and hate burning within.

What do you think that does to a person?

Do you think it really affects the person who "Wronged" them?

They don't seem to realize that, no matter the wrong done, the other person didn't "Make" them angry, and that they can choose to let go of the anger.

Yes, anger happens. It can happen quickly and is rooted in other emotions like sadness and loss and helplessness. But you can always choose how deeply you let it affect you.

If you're holding onto anger I encourage you to let it go. Release it. Free yourself to experience the other wonderful emotions of life.

I promise you'll be glad you did.

One More Breath

This is the true story of how listening to my inner voice—call it The Spirit, a Hunch, Intuition, or whatever you'd like—allowed me to make a difference. I hope reading it encourages you to pay attention to your inner voice so you can be the miracle for someone in need.

This happened over six years ago. But I remember it like it was yesterday.

One More Breath

Run!

What..?

Why did I have the overwhelming urge to run? I was barefoot, in swimming trunks, and walking through a crowded pedestrian plaza.

Run!

A voice shouted in my head. I shrugged and started running toward the resort pool.

Earlier, I was at the pool with my children when my 21-month-old son began rubbing his eyes and whining. He needed a nap. Since fatigue and water are a dangerous combination I took him to mommy. I was returning to the pool when the urge to Run hit me.

FASTER..!

Without question I sprinted the last hundred yards, only slowing enough to navigate the pool's entry.

Part 1: Transformations

Once inside I shrugged--that was weird. Then I felt I should go to the outside portion of the pool.

So I did.

I was looking for a small diving ring--the kind of toy that can keep kids, and me, occupied for hours. We were missing one and I wanted to find it.

I walked around the right side of the pool, carefully scanning the water for signs of the wayward plastic ring.

No luck.

I'd covered most of the pool's perimeter and was getting ready to look in the covered section when I saw something strange. A little boy was floating in the middle of the pool. Odd, he looked still, too still, and was bobbing gently. His skin was blue, almost purple...

He was drowning!

I jumped in and grabbed him. My only thought; I've got to get the water out of his lungs! I placed my right hand in the middle of his stomach, grasped him firmly by the shoulder, and then lifted him above my head while keeping his body's weight centered on my right hand.

Success! Water gushed from his mouth.

I had to get him out of the pool--so I could continue working. The water seemed thick, like syrup sticking to my limbs, as I fought my way to the edge. But I made it.

I yelled for someone to hold him while I climbed out. A young woman came over and took him. I got out, grabbed him back from her, and went to work.

I've had a lot of training--CPR, First Responder--but it had been so long and I'm ashamed to say I hadn't renewed my certifications. In retrospect I can think of many things I did wrong...but luckily I did enough right.

Another Slice of Pi

I turned him over, holding his head slightly lower than his body, and pounded his back a few more times--to make sure all of the water was out of his lungs. Then I noticed a small crowd around me and remembered...911!

"Someone call 911!" I hollered. Then screamed, "Someone call 911!"

A woman, his mother I learned later, took his head and gave him a few breaths--CPR. His color returned slightly, but he was still unconscious. I couldn't work on him properly if he was in my lap, so I placed him on the nearest table and tried to listen for breathing. I couldn't hear or feel anything. So I tilted his head back, plugged his nose, and gave him *one more breath*. I felt it go in. I tried to listen again, but there was too much noise.

"Everybody quiet!" I shouted. I had to see if he was breathing. I thought I heard him inhale, but I had to be sure.

He took in a breath and whimpered like a newborn. Then he drew a deeper breath and seemed to gain strength. I held him until I was sure he wasn't going to quit breathing and then handed him to his mom. By that time he was crying, crying weakly, but crying.

I stepped back and waited for the ambulance to arrive, a world lifting from my shoulders.

I've never been comfortable with recognition or praise and this time was no different. If I hadn't known the medics would want to question me, I'd have bolted. Instead, I sucked it up and waited.

In the interim, people kept coming up to me and saying things like, "They don't realize yet what you've done for them today." Or, "You're the hero of the day." I shrugged these off as

Part 1: Transformations

gracefully as I could. I didn't care about being a hero. I didn't want to be a hero. I only wanted him to be alright.

I answered the medics' questions and then gathered my children. On the way out I told on of the medics what room I was in--in case they needed anything else--and asked if the little boy was going to be ok. They told me he should...

Later that night I learned his name. And that he'd spent the rest of the day at Primary Children's Hospital. He was unharmed; no brain damage or other ill effects would plague him.

The next day I meet him and his parents. They are wonderful people. They were very gracious and--though it was unnecessary--thanked me profusely. He is three years old--a year older than my son--with ice blue eyes and blond hair. He's full of energy and just a little shy.

I'll always remember the day I helped save his life. Maybe someday I'll tell you how he helped save mine.

End

Remember always; Listen! *Be The Miracle!*

Declaration for Success! (For Men)

This is your declaration to yourself that you are successful. Print it. Read it with feeling then sign and date it. Now post it somewhere that you can see it often during the day.

Every morning *read Your Declaration for Success* with feeling before you start your day!

Your subconscious mind will handle the rest.

Declaration for Success!

I AM A MAN OF ACTION!

Done are the days of sitting by waiting for life to bring me the things I desire.

I make things happen! I use my energy and my actions to *manifest Grand Results*! I *am* the person I want to be! Every day I *am stronger* and *wiser* and more *adept at producing the results I desire in life*!

I live by the motto: "Be, Do, Have!"

I follow the formula $T+F+A=R$ *every day!*

I learn from failures and turn them into success!

I am a Man of Action!

My Thoughts are *Powerful, Positive,* and *Productive*!

My Feelings are *Powerful, Positive,* and *Productive*!

My Actions are *Inspired, Powerful,* and *Massively Productive*!

Part 1: Transformations

From this day forth I take *Massive, Inspired Action & I create the life of my dreams!*

I AM A MAN OF ACTION!

Signature:_____

Date:_____

You Are the Master of Your Destiny

Download and print your Declaration here:
http://www.rolandbyrd.co/ynbp/extras/Declaration_Men.pdf

Another Slice of Pi

Declaration for Success! (For Women)

This is your declaration to yourself that you are successful. Print it. Read it with feeling then sign and date it. Now post it somewhere that you can see it often during the day.

Every morning *read Your Declaration for Success* with feeling before you start your day!

Your subconscious mind will handle the rest.

Declaration for Success!

I AM A WOMAN OF ACTION!

Done are the days of sitting by waiting for life to bring me the things I desire.

I make things happen! I use my energy and my actions to *manifest Grand Results*! I *am* the person I want to be! Every day I *am stronger* and *wiser* and more *adept at producing the results I desire in life*!

I live by the motto: "Be, Do, Have!"

I follow the formula *$T+F+A=R$ every day!*

I learn from failures and turn them into success!

I am a Woman of Action!

My Thoughts are *Powerful, Positive, and Productive!*

My Feelings are *Powerful, Positive, and Productive!*

Part 1: Transformations

My Actions are *Inspired, Powerful, and Massively Productive!*

From this day forth I take *Massive, Inspired Action & I create the life of my dreams!*

I AM A WOMAN OF ACTION!
Signature:_____
Date:_____
You Are the Master of Your Destiny!

Download and print your Declaration here:
http://www.rolandbyrd.co/ynbp/extras/Declaration_Women.pdf

T+F+A=R (An Equation for Life!)

What's the equation for all the results you get in life?

It's simple.

Thoughts + Feelings + Actions = Results

That's: **T+F+A=R**

Everything you do starts with a thought. Even if you're unaware of the thought it's there. The things you think about most—consciously and subconsciously—shape the things you do the most. Choose thoughts that align with who your true self and your actions will align accordingly.

Feelings, especially powerful feelings, tell your mind something is important. The more important it is the more you'll think about it. Strong emotions also guide the Law of Attraction. Remember, Thoughts and Feelings are causally related and affect each other in a circular fashion. Clarify your emotions and use them to tell your subconscious mind what's important to you. Then your thoughts and feelings will adjust accordingly.

Actions make things happen. The results of actions may be desirable or undesirable but they are always there. Understand; taking no action is an action and will produce results just as doing something that moves you toward your dreams is an action that will produce results. Open your mind to the possibilities of life. Then take inspired action. It's a magical combination.

Part 1: Transformations

Learn to guide your Thoughts, to use your Emotions, and to take action and you'll realize amazing results in your life!

If you'd like assistance with this process, get a copy of [Your Blueprint Life by Design](#) today! It's chock full of great resources that empower you to take control of your life.

Life is a Mirror

One of the things I've learned over the past few years is that *Life is a Mirror*.

The condition of your life reflects your subconscious beliefs and the condition of your soul. People with chaotic lives have chaotic subconscious beliefs. Their souls are in turmoil. People whose lives are filled with pain or violence have subconscious beliefs that pain or violence is necessary to their existence. On some level pain or violence fulfills their needs and validates their existence.

Conversely, those who have happy, peaceful, ordered lives have subconscious beliefs about life being happy, peaceful, and ordered. The manifestation of these subconscious beliefs validates the existence of the beliefs and of the individual.

The realization that your life is a reflection of your subconscious beliefs is painful at times. After all, few people—especially those who are unhappy with their life—like to realize that the condition of their life is their responsibility.

But it is.

Yes, it's true that sometimes horrible things happen in life. It's true that you often have little control over what happens to you. You aren't able to control others actions. And that's an easy way to redirect accountability, to say it's not my responsibility. But the powerful truth is that you can always *choose how you respond* to what happens in your life. You can choose to make something wonderful or something catastrophic out of anything that happens to you.

And so the power of responsibility comes right back to you.

The beautiful thing about understanding that your life is your responsibility is that it gives you the power to change it!

You have the power to change your subconscious beliefs. You have the power to change the reflection of your life's mirror.

So what are you going to do?

In the end a mirror is a wonderful tool. It shows, by reflection, what's working and what isn't. Once you understand that truth, *you will change your life*.

Happy 4th of July!

Have a great 4th of July!

Even if you're not from the USA, today is a great day to celebrate Freedom!

You have the freedom to choose the path of your life!
You have the freedom to choose happiness!
You have the freedom to create the life of your dreams!
You have the freedom to unlock your true potential!
Celebrate these freedoms by taking action today!
Take charge of your life. Start today!
You Are the Master of Your Destiny!

Part 1: Transformations

Absolutes

Have you ever used words like "Never" and "Always" when talking about something you don't know how to do?

They are black and white words used to describe a world full of marvelous colors.

I call words like that Absolutes because they lock the current state—or behavior—as the way it will always be. They are limiting and can be damaging to your psyche. Using them—when speaking about things you don't know how to do—is like locking your subconscious mind in a dungeon. It practically guarantees you'll never succeed.

And let's get real here; whether you say, "I'll never be able to...", "I'll never get it...", "I always mess up...." or any other phrase of that nature, what you're really saying is, "I Can't".

"I can't" is one of the most limiting phrases in the world. Knowing that, why would you ever say it?

Now take this a little further.

Have you ever said to your partner or children or friends, "You Always..." or "You'll Never..." when you felt upset about something?

When you think about it, is that a true statement?

Is it possible for a person—regardless of age—to "Always" act one way, to "Never" get something, or "Never" change their behavior?

Always and Never... That's a long time. Longer I dare say than any of us will walk this Earth.

Another Slice of Pi

When people hear they'll "Always" or "Never" enough times from people they care about, they start to believe it. This is especially true for children. Many people grow up with severely limiting beliefs about their capabilities and worth because of things they were repeatedly told as children.

The good news is that we are dynamic, flexible beings and can change this programming once we're aware of it.

The even better news is that, knowing this, you make the choice to avoid absolutes when speaking to people in your life. Help them believe in themselves by believing in them first.

Part 1: Transformations

Happiness

It's no secret; few things in life bring more happiness than releasing your ego and helping others. So when I came across this Chinese Proverb the other day I immediately thought of you.

If you want happiness for an hour, take a nap.
If you want happiness for a day, go fishing.
If you want happiness for a year, inherit a fortune.
If you want happiness for a lifetime, help somebody.

Like everything in life, happiness is a choice. You can choose to feel happy regardless of your circumstances. That might sound strange. But if you seek it, if you look, there is always a reason to find happiness because there is always something good in everything. I've also found that the happier I am, the more I have to give. The more I have to give, the happier I am. That's a nice feedback loop to be in. :-)

Choose to help others. You might be their light in the darkness. You may be their reason to give it another go. You might be the Miracle they need. Even something as simple as a kind word, when spoken to a person in need, can have life changing impact.

So make the choice today to have and share happiness and miracles with your life.

Another Slice of Pi

Is Your Past an Anchor?

Is Your Past Holding You Back?

I was talking with some friends the other night and the topic of dealing with the past came up. Some people feel like the past is an anchor weighing them down. They feel the mistakes they've made define who they are.

I used to feel that way too.

The problem with that thinking is it gives away your power to make a difference in your life or anyone else's. It places you square in the middle of the victim mentality because you allow yourself to become the victim of your past choices.

When a person fixates on their past, especially the mistakes they've made, their past becomes an anchor. Their progress stops and they sit frozen in a fluid world.

Instead of holding onto past mistakes and using them to punish yourself, use those mistakes as the rudder that keeps you on course. Use the mistakes as lessons—After all, you're attending the University of Life. Look at them long enough to figure out what you must do differently in the future. Then look ahead again and do thing differently!

Armed with the knowledge you've gained you'll avoid pitfalls you might otherwise fall into.

Realize this is true of little mistakes as well as huge ones. Many people allow small mistakes to pile up in their minds until they have a mountain of errors hanging over their heads. Shift your focus and that mountain becomes the climb leading

Part 1: Transformations

to the amazing view of the future. Those mistakes become lessons and ultimately the building blocks of success.

Here are a few steps to help you get started:

Start by learning the lessons an event in the past holds for you.

Apply those lessons in your life.

Forgive others and forgive yourself.

So what are you going to do?

Your past is your past. It's unchangeable, locked in the fabric of time. What you do with your past is completely up to you. I challenge you to change your focus, learn from your life, and get out there and do something wonderful!

How to Develop Gratitude!

Are You Grateful?

In the past there were times I felt I had no reason to be grateful. I felt like everything was going wrong, like I couldn't do anything right. There are many problems with that type of thinking. One of the biggest is the self-defeating spiral it creates.

If you feel ungrateful, you notice things you're ungrateful about. The more you notice things you feel ungrateful about, the more ungrateful you feel...

That's a sad place to live.

But... When *you feel grateful*, you *notice things you're grateful about*. Then *you feel even more grateful*. Then you *notice even more that you're grateful about* and you *feel more and more grateful!*

That's an Awesome Place to Live!

I'm very grateful I learned about the Power of Gratitude!

But what if your gratitude muscles are a weak? How do you develop them?

One of the best tools I've learned for strengthening gratitude is to keep a Gratitude Journal. It's a quick and easy way to start noticing all of the great things in your life.

Just take a small notebook—any notebook will do—and before you go to bed at night write ten things you're grateful for in your Gratitude Journal. It's best when you write things that happened that day—that you're grateful for—because it reminds you of the wonderful things happening in your life right now. But if you have to write something basic like; "I'm grateful that I have air to breathe." Or, "I'm grateful I have water to drink." That's OK too!

Start where you are and *build those Gratitude Muscles!*

When you *Do This*, you'll notice a change in your perception of life. You'll *feel happier*. You'll *be kinder*. You'll *experience more abundance*. Then you'll wonder why you ever wasted time feeling ungrateful.

For more tips on how to change your focus and your life, Read [Your Blueprint, Life by Design](#)!

Falling Down

Do you ever let little things get in the way of important things?

Sometimes I do.

Earlier this year I stopped exercising. It wasn't an overnight decision. It was a process of finding small reasons to put each workout off. Before I knew it I'd gone two and a half months without exercising!

In the past—before I learned that I was 100% accountable for my life—I would have felt like a failure. That would have become a self-fulfilling prophecy and whammo! I'd still be lamenting the things that "Got in the way" of my working out. I'd have gone into a downward spiral and would still sit here wondering why I didn't have time to exercise.

Instead I stopped and thought, "This isn't working... What can I do to make time to exercise again?" I brainstormed about it and came up with three simple answers.

Go to bed earlier.

Get up in time and exercise to start my day.

Start!

So I started doing those three easy things. Now I've been exercising again for five months. And it's easy because exercising is habit I've had for almost seven years now.

This is true of everything in life. Sometimes we let little things get in the way of important things. "Urgent" gets handled whether or not it's "Important" and "Important" things that don't seem "Urgent" fall to the side.

Part 1: Transformations

That's the "Crisis Mode" of management. It only works for so long, because everything Important becomes Urgent when ignored long enough.

I challenge you to ask yourself, "Is there something important in my life that I've been putting off?"

If the answer is yes that's OK. Today's the perfect day to *start doing it*!

It's also important to remember that you can choose your way out of a good habit...But you can just as easily *choose your way back into it*.

MindKiDo—The Art of Mental Redirection

If you're like most people, unwelcome thoughts enter your head at times. And most people deal with those thoughts by trying to force them from their mind.

But there's a problem with that method. Trying to force thoughts from your mind makes them stronger. This happens because forcing a thought from your mind takes a lot of mental energy. You end up focusing on the unwanted thought. Focusing on the unwanted thought tells your subconscious mind the thought is important. So it starts bringing it to mind more often. In fact, the harder you push a thought away, the more often it comes back.

If you don't believe this concept then take a few minutes and actively force any thoughts of the color Blue from your mind. Every time you think of Blue you must force it away, tell yourself you can't think of Blue. When you're done with the exercise come back and read the rest of this.

.1-

Understand; you have to think the unwanted thought to think of forcing it from your mind. And realize that your subconscious mind is much stronger than your conscious mind. Not only are you thinking the unwanted thought when you force it from your mind but your subconscious plays tricks on you too. Things like popping the unwanted thought into your

Part 1: Transformations

mind—so you can make sure you're not thinking it... Yeah, the subconscious mind is a sneaky bugger!

Sound hopeless?

Far from it!

You can rid yourself of unwanted thoughts by using the art of mental redirection. Instead of forcing a thought from your mind just start thinking of something else. Give no energy to the unwanted thought. Let it flow out of your mind naturally while replacing it with a thought you want. When you *do this* as habit, unwanted thoughts become self-defeating because they automatically trigger thoughts you want.

Call it MindKiDo!

For more great ideas about reshaping your thought processes *and* how to use your subconscious mind as an ally **read** *"Your Blueprint, Life by Design" and "Break Your Mold: The Art of Overcoming Patterns and Behaviors That Hold You Back"*.

http://www.rolandbyrd.co/books-by-roland-byrd/

How to Play Bigger in Life

Have you ever wanted something from life that felt out of reach?

What did you do?

Did you take action and do everything you could to make it happen?

Or did you give up on your dream and then lie to yourself? You know what I mean. Did you convince yourself that you never wanted that dream anyway? It was a foolish dream...

If you took the first path I imagine you either succeeded or found something even better. If you took the second path, which most people do, then you probably just went on with a hollow spot in your heart.

I was part of the majority for most of my life. I played small. I was a champion quitter.

Why?

Sometime during my childhood I learned to play small. I learned that standing out in the crowd was bad. I learned it was easier to quit before I started something than to risk failing or worse...embarrassing myself. And I spent a good part of my life living that way.

I tried to be invisible.

This personal experience sums it up. I was on the wrestling team in high school. I was a senior and came back to wrestling after taking two years off to focus on weight training. I was strong and had the unrealistic expectation that my

Part 1: Transformations

strength was enough to make me a champion wrestler. I didn't realize I lacked the skill that came from consistent applied effort and training.

During the wrestle-offs—where we wrestled for rank in our weight class—I lost to both guys in my weight class. I was out classed. Even a sophomore, who wasn't nearly as strong as me, pinned me.

If that happened to me today I'd think, "OK. Looks like you've got some work to do." Then I'd figure out how to wrestle better. I'd practice. I'd learn and I'd fight for what I wanted. But back then...I did the thing I'd learned best. I quit the team and convinced myself that I really didn't want to wrestle. I'd rather just weight train.

That was playing small. That was lying to myself.

But the problem is if you want anything from life—other than a fast trip to Mediocrity's Oblivion—you'd better play bigger!

Playing Big means stepping outside your comfort zone. It means taking action. It means doing things that might look crazy to others but that make your heart sing! Most of all, Playing Big means believing in your dreams and doing everything you can to make them happen.

That might sound alien to you. If it does, that's OK. Here are some things you can do to Start Playing Bigger.

Write down your dream.

Put it someplace you can see it and read it every day.

Take inspired action—when you're thinking about your dream and something pops into your head do it!

Do at least one thing every day that moves you closer to your dream!

Another Slice of Pi

For easy to follow guide books that teach you how to Play Bigger and how to create success in your life, *Read "Your Blueprint, Life by Design" and "Break Your Mold: The Art of Overcoming Patterns and Behaviors That Hold You Back".*

http://www.rolandbyrd.co/books-by-roland-byrd/

Part 1: Transformations

Unconditional Love

What is Unconditional Love?

To me unconditional love means loving a person no matter what they do. This doesn't mean you must agree with or like the choices they make, nor does it mean you expose yourself to harm. It means you love them and are unwilling to let personal feelings—about their choices—interfere with your love.

In my childhood I learned conditional love. I'm sure my parents loved me despite choices I made. Or at least in my fantasy they did. But the displays of love I received were often related to what I did or didn't do or to how I behaved. So I learned that love was withdrawn when I did something wrong.

As you can imagine this was the root of a many problems in my life.

I also acted that way myself without realizing it for most of my life. Meaning I withdrew emotionally when I felt unhappy or hurt. I didn't consciously do this to remove love from others. It was to protect myself by creating walls of numbness around my heart. But the end result was a withdrawal of love. That's counterproductive to say the least.

I've learned now that I must open myself to all emotions to be a whole person. This means opening myself to hurt and pain when I experience them as well as opening myself to love and joy. *It is only by opening ourselves to all emotions that we fully experience life.* Also, there is something in letting an emotion wash over you that prevents it from taking root. Emotions are temporary by nature. In fact, emotions are illusions we create to give meaning to the events in our lives. Or perhaps it is better said that emotions are the result of our present reality getting filtered through our history—which happens all the time.

I believe the only emotion that is truly tied to the now is Joy. When we get rid of all the other things we filter life through and live in the pure moment, we are in joy.

If you've found you're drifting from love with someone close to you, try this exercise for a few weeks.

Each day, before you go to bed, take a piece of paper and write down ten things you love or appreciate about this person. Even if it's something like, "I love that they have a good sense of style." Write it down.

As you *Do This* you'll find each day you discover more things about the person that you appreciate and love.

Everyone has good qualities. Everyone has things worth loving. Everyone is worth loving.

Love is a choice. *Choose love.*

Part 1: Transformations

Do You Know Who You Are?

Lately I've been asking myself, "Who am I?" I know who I am but seek greater insight and understanding. I'm looking past the labels I've imposed on myself over the years—or have chosen to let others impose on me.

For each person the process of discovering "Who am I?" is a unique and personal journey. Through meditation these are the answers I've received.

Who am I?
I am creation.
I am choice.
I am infinite possibility.
I am nothing.
I am everything.
I am the collapsing of all probability waves into this beautiful moment.

As with all questions of this type, there are no right or wrong answers. There are simply, "Answers".

I ask those of you who read this, "Who are you?"

I encourage you to gift yourself the time to reflect on this question. Your answers might surprise you.

You Are The Master of Your Destiny!

What do You Believe about Your Physical Capabilities?

Do you believe you're weak?

Do you limit yourself because of an injury?

Do you label yourself clumsy?

What you tell yourself about your capabilities is a self-fulfilling prophecy. So if you're telling yourself how clumsy, slow, or weak you are, STOP!

Start telling yourself that *You are* more *capable. You are* more *graceful. You are* more *adept. You are stronger.*

No matter where you are now physically, *you can improve*. Even my wife's grandmother—who in her late 80's hadn't walked in years—started walking with a walker once she believed she could.

If she can do it, You Can Do It!

Part 1: Transformations

Act on Inspiration!

Whatever your craft, trade, hobby, or art form *you will receive inspiration*. Inspiration is a gift. Your duty is to act on inspiration!

If you choose to leave inspiration alone, in time you'll receive less and less inspiration. But when you *Act on It*, when you say, "Wow! What a great idea!" and then do something with your inspiration...

That's when magic happens.

Using an example from my life; I wrote the bulk of my first book, *Your Blueprint, Life by Design*, in about 2.5 weeks. I wrote it by inspiration and I believe the book is much more than I could have created on my own—meaning without inspiration.

My second book—that I just finished writing a few days ago—was written in less than three weeks too. Like the first, I wrote it by inspiration. I was meditating one morning when the idea appeared in my mind and I knew I had to run with it, to take immediate action. So I donated most of my free time over the next few weeks to creating the book. Then one morning it was done. My second book...done, finished! What an amazing feeling.

Whatever your desire, whatever your craft, you have the ability to receive inspiration. Dare I say you're entitled to it?

I believe you are.

Another Slice of Pi

The first step is to ask for inspiration. The second step is to Act on It!

Go ahead, give it a try. What have you got to lose?

Part 1: Transformations

Remembering 9/11/01

Where were you on Sept 11, 2001?

Chances are you remember it clearly. I worked as a delivery driver and was at one of my morning stops, a gas station, when I looked over and saw a news flash on the TV. An unthinkable image met my eyes. One of the Twin Towers was smoking.

Horrified at the tragic image and wondering what was going on, I stood riveted to the floor and watched. I heard snippets of conversation around me and understanding slowly dawned. Someone had deliberately flown a plane into one of the Twin Towers!

Then the second tower was struck...

In that moment life changed for all of us, for the whole world but especially for Americans. We lived in varying degrees of shock over the next few weeks and months. Shock turned to outrage. Outrage led to action. For a time it brought the people of the USA closer together than they'd been in years.

Here we are. Ten years later. Many things have changed, some for the better, some not. But as a country the US survived. As a world we have survived.

Please give a moment of silent reverence today to the victims of 911, to their families, and to all the people this tragic act impacted.

Then go on living. *Be the miracle you desire in this world!*

Do You Say, "I Can't..."

Have you ever said, "I can't..."?

I know I used to say that. What I didn't know then was how much that simple phrase limited my life.

I remember in high school when I thought, "I can't bench press more than 250lbs." I spent a year fighting that limit I'd placed on myself. Then one day I thought, "What if I can?"

Within a few months of my mental shift I was benching 315lbs for 3 sets of 5 reps.

Then there was the time I thought, "I can't use a window squeegee with my right hand because of nerve damage..." Sure enough, I dropped it every time I tried. But I had to learn how to use the squeegee or I was out of a job! So I learned it left handed.

For months I cleaned windows with my left hand—I'm right handed. Then one day I thought, "What if I can clean windows right handed despite my nerve damage?" I placed the squeegee in my right hand and cleaned the window with flawless form. And from then on I've been near ambidextrous.

By the time I started martial arts I'd learned a little bit about Can't and Can. I was in my early twenties and had never seriously trained before. I wanted to do the splits, both ways. People kept telling me, "You can't do the splits. You're too old."

I said, "Watch me."

It took almost two years for me to figure it out. But I got my splits both ways—totally flat to the ground.

Part 1: Transformations

"Yes I can!"

I'm sure you've had times when you thought, "I can't..." we all have. But the truth is "I can't" usually means one of two things:

I don't want to.

I don't know how

Neither of those really means can't. Can't is something like breathing in outer space without a space suit or breathing apparatus.

So let's all do ourselves a favor and drop that word from our vocabulary.

If you don't want to, say, "I don't want to."

If you don't know how, say, "I don't know how." And the best thing about not knowing how to do something is this:

You can learn! If you really want to...you'll figure it out.

Careful… Your Subconscious Beliefs are Showing!

How do your Subconscious Beliefs affect your life?

I remember one time when I was seventeen; I was hiking in the mountains with a few friends. We walked up a steep hill and I had to stop every twenty feet or so to catch my breath.

My friends teased me because I was lean and muscular and looked like I was in great shape on the outside. The problem was I had no endurance because I'd trained my body with low reps, heavy weight, and lots of rest between sets.

That's ok if all you want is large muscles. But it's a poor combination for overall fitness.

And to make it worse I smoked, chewed tobacco, and drank tons of coffee and soda.

Basically I was the poster child for how to abuse your body but still look like you're fit.

I didn't understand that my body had to last my entire life. I know, it sounds silly. But I was guilty of the same immortality complex that many youth have.

The problem wasn't with my workout routine or my habits though. They were problems. But they weren't "The Problem".

The Problem was with my Subconscious Beliefs about being "In Shape" and with my Subconscious Beliefs about what "Physically Fit" meant. In my Subconscious Mind I believed that physical fitness was all about how good I looked

Part 1: Transformations

without a shirt. Forget whole body fitness or cardiovascular work! My subconscious belief system didn't include anything about functional fitness or bodyweight exercises either. I believed that pumping cold, hard iron was the only way to build muscle.

So what happened?

By the time I was in my early thirties I'd ballooned to 230lbs. of jiggling, unsightly FAT! Forget taking my shirt off in public. I was even embarrassed for my wife to see me without my shirt!

And then came the day that a doctor told me I was, "Grossly Obese..." I didn't think that was fair because I *only* weighed 235lbs. And by society's standards I was overweight but not obese! But the doctor was talking about a medical point of view and according to the body mass index I was "Grossly Obese." Besides, at just over 5ft 9in tall, 235lbs. of non-muscled mass is unsightly and very unhealthy.

I listened to the doctor and decided I had to do something about my weight and overall health. But I'd tried working out during the years since high school and it always seemed to end the same way. I'd decide to "Get In Shape" and start going to the gym. Then I'd work out like a maniac for 2 to 2.5 hours a day 6 days a week.

That might work when you're young and single but for a married dad it's problematic to maintain that kind of schedule. But as you understand, that was my Subconscious Mind's Beliefs about fitness manifesting!

So to keep from taking time away from my family I'd exercise first thing in the morning before I went to work. But, as you imagine, I never kept that up for long. I'd usually make it about 6 months—just long enough to see a real difference in my physique before burning out and starting to miss workouts. And once I started missing workouts I'd miss more and more until I wasn't working out at all.

And the cycle went round and round.

Something clicked after that doctor told me I was "Grossly Obese" though. I realized I'd better change my method because *my method obviously wasn't working.*

A few days later I had an epiphany. I decided I'd stop trying to "Get In Shape" and start trying to *live a fitness lifestyle* instead. That was a massive subconscious shift. I stopped worrying about how much weight I could bench press or squat and started to *focus on being healthy.* I decided to *make healthy choices and have functional fitness.* I started training with [bodyweight exercises](), which exercise muscle groups instead of specific muscles. That was another tremendous shift for my Subconscious Mind.

As you realize, I'd dramatically changed my subconscious mind's beliefs about what fitness is. The power in my new Subconscious Beliefs gave me lasting purpose and helped me develop a fitness lifestyle instead of bouncing from one a temporary fitness goal to another.

The end result of my new subconscious beliefs was that I went from 235lbs to 175lbs within six months! And the best part is that since then—nearly 7 years ago now—I've stayed healthy and fit and kept exercising on a regular basis because overall health and fitness is now my lifestyle!

Part 1: Transformations

Are You Ready to Be The Miracle?

How can you Be The Miracle?

I'm sure you've heard the phrase, "Be The Miracle." But what does it mean? After all, don't we all have differing ideas of what a miracle is?

These are the two most common definitions of Miracle from Merriam Webster's

1 : an extraordinary event manifesting divine intervention in human affairs

2 : an extremely outstanding or unusual event, thing, or accomplishment

I imagine you're thinking, "Great. Now I know the definition but that doesn't answer the question, 'How can I Be The miracle?'..."

Fair enough.

Aren't you both of those?

The very fact that you exist is a Miracle. Seriously, what are the odds that the exact combination of DNA would come together at the exact moment necessary to create you? What are the odds that all of the experiences in your life would happen in the sequence they did to shape you? What are the odds that you'd grow and learn and evolve into the person you are?

You are a perfect creation of God! Isn't that a Miracle?

Another Slice of Pi

I know you might not feel like a perfect creation of God. You might not feel like a Miracle. You might not like yourself. You might think you've had a crappy life and wonder how that can possibly be a Miracle?

Because you're here and you have the power to choose! Because your life is unfolding before you and you have the power to shape it! Because God doesn't make mistakes!

No matter what's happened in your life, regardless of the mistakes you've made, the people who've hurt you, or even the triumphs you've experienced and the people who've loved you unconditionally, you have the power to choose!

You have the power to learn and grow!

You have the power to evolve!

No one's future is etched in stone. Your future is a sea of endless possibilities. So start captaining your life and set course for your dreams!

Gandhi said, "We must be the change we wish to see in the world." That means you must Be The Miracle you wish to see in your life. As you learn to do this it also helps you Be The Miracle in the lives of others.

There are many things you can do to be a miracle in your life and the lives of others.

If you're unhappy with your life you can **START MAKING BETTER CHOICES.** The choices you make today shape tomorrow. They shape tomorrow for you and those close to you. That's one way to Be The Miracle!

You can look inside and **DISCOVER WHAT SUBCONSCIOUS BELIEFS ARE LIMITING YOU.** Your Subconscious Mind has more power than you might imagine. Roughly 90% of your thoughts happen subconsciously. Yet those subconscious thoughts are the Blueprint for Your Life. To figure out what your subconscious beliefs are just look at the condition of your life. Your Subconscious Beliefs aren't what you want consciously; they're what you're getting in reality. That's the Power of your Subconscious Mind!

You can **FORGIVE YOURSELF.** That might sound bizarre but most of us are our own worst critics. Who wants to do something for someone that's constantly putting them down? So stop putting yourself down, forgive yourself for past mistakes and make the choices necessary to avoid those mistakes in the future.

You can **CHANGE YOUR FOCUS.** What you focus on is what you'll find. The person who hates thorns will see the thorns in a rosebush while the person who loves roses will only see the flowers. That's the power of your subconscious mind! So make the choice today to see your life through new eyes. Start looking for Miracles. Start seeing the beauty and love and joy that's all around you. Start looking for what you want and you'll find more of it!

Another powerful way to Be The Miracle is to realize that though things will happen over which you have no control, **YOU ALWAYS CONTROL YOUR RESPONSE.** You can always choose what to do with any situation or event in your life. I challenge you to find the good in every event and to start responding to life instead of reacting to it.

Learn to Be The Miracle in Your Life and Become The Miracle in the Lives of Others!

Have you ever felt like you had nothing left to give?

I'm sure you have. We've all felt that way at some time or another. But what causes it and how can you move past it?

Feeling like you've nothing left to give can come from a few different places. It can be caused by not meeting your basic needs—I'll come back to that. It can also be caused by selfishness. A selfish person is afraid of losing their time or giving things away because they're afraid they won't get them back. The problem with that is we're designed to act as conduits. We get more from life when we exchange than we do when we hoard.

Think of time and things as the air you breathe. If you lock yourself in an air tight room—because you're afraid of giving up any of "your air" you'll eventually die of asphyxiation. But if you stand outside and breathe freely, you're exchanging "your air" with all of the plants and animals on our planet. The animals take out oxygen and produce carbon dioxide, true, but the plants take out carbon dioxide and produce oxygen. It's a beautiful balance, a miracle of engineering that allows animals and plants to participate in a free flowing exchange vital to life.

The same is true of your time, energy, and other resources. If you hoard them you're selling yourself short because you're not participating in the exchange vital to life. Sure

Part 1: Transformations

you'll get more time—everyone does—and you might get more stuff, but you won't flourish because you're taking instead of exchanging.

But if you share your time, energy, and resources, you're part of the exchange. As you give more, you not only help others but you allow others to help you by opening space in your life to receive. Remember this exchange is vital to others as well as you. Sharing your time, energy, and resources often allows you to be the miracle in other's lives.

So, what does that have to do with being The Miracle in Your Life?

Great question!

We all have basic needs. If our basic needs aren't met we aren't able to care for ourselves or others. I'm sure you've heard the adage, "A drowning person can't save anyone." If you're drowning emotionally, spiritually, psychologically, or physically you'll never effectively help others because you're too concerned with your own survival. And that's how it should be.

You must survive!

So to be the miracle in your life, you must figure out how to meet your basic needs. Only then can you effectively help others and become a miracle in their lives.

But isn't that selfish, to put your own needs above another?

That depends on the needs.

If all of your basic needs—food, clothing, shelter, etc.—are met and you choose to ignore others needs then that's probably selfish. But if you aren't able to meet your own basic needs and you're giving away things that could provide stability... Is that really the best choice?

Another Slice of Pi

I know it gets a little sticky here.

The best way I can say it is this: If you want to be the miracle in others' lives, figure out how you want to help. Then figure out what you must do to exceed your basic needs in that area of life and give from your excess. In other words, Figure out how to be The Miracle in your life so you can be the Miracle in the lives of others!

Does that make sense?

If you want to help financially, then figure out how to make more money than you need to meet your needs and wants and give from the extra. After all what good does it do to give away money if you lose your home in the process or you can't eat? But people like Bono or Steve Jobs (RIP) or Oprah give away more money than many will make in ten lifetimes *and* they still have plenty left over!

If you want to help emotionally then figure out how to meet your basic emotional needs and give from the excess!

If you want to help by donating your time then figure out how to best manage your time so you meet all of your time needs and still have excess to donate!

If you want to donate by giving physical service then figure out how to meet all of your body's needs so you have extra energy and strength to donate!

Today I challenge you to figure out how to meet your basic needs! *Learn to be the Miracle in your life!* The go and *be the miracle in the lives of others!*

Part 1: Transformations

Do You Know What Your Passion is?

How To Discover Your Passion!

One of the most important things that will improve your ability to succeed in life--and financially--is to discover your passion and do it!

But you can't figure out how to use your passion to help others, and make money, until you know what it is.

How do you know what your passion is? I mean, sure... there are things you enjoy doing, but are they things *you're really passionate about*?

Sometimes it is hard to know the difference between a true passion and something that's a temporary flash of excitement. Emotions can be misleading. What feels like passion today might not be your *true passion*.

Have heart though, because there are a few sure-fire ways to tell the difference between plain excitement and real passion.

First, *you must figure out what your passions are.*

If you want to discover your passion, then keep reading. But I warn you, this takes a little work. So if you really don't care what your passion is...you might want to skip the rest of this message. But if you really, really want to figure that magical activity that makes you giddy with glee, that ignites the fire in your soul, that aligns destiny with your purpose in life... *Then Keep Reading!*

Another Slice of Pi

The first thing I'd like you to do is take a piece of blank paper and write "My Passions" on the top of it—if you need to use more than one piece that's okay too. Now think of the top ten things you most enjoy doing and write them down. Make sure you leave an inch or two free underneath each item. They don't need to be in any particular order either. The important thing is to get them on the page.

Go ahead and do it now.

*
*
*
*
*
*
*
*
*
*
*
*
*
*
*
*
*
*

Are you done?

Good.

Now take another piece of paper and write this:

"I would love to _____ !"

Part 1: Transformations

Fill in the blank with each passion you wrote down and read it out loud.

Do this for every passion on your list. Pay attention to your feelings when you read the statement, listen to them. At least one of the passions you've listed will make your heart sing!

Which ones give you a jolt of happiness when you read them? Mark these with a star.

Now you have your list of passions and you've separated them into two groups. The group that you didn't put stars by are still things you'll want to do. They are things you enjoy. They aren't your real passions though. And that means you might have a harder time staying motivated about them.

The items with stars are your passions. Motivation is easier with these because you love doing them! But which one of them is The One, the Passion that carries your life to the next level and does the most good in the process?

Here's how you find out.

I'll use this sample list:

Exercise

Singing

Dancing

Quilting

Writing

Start with each one and compare it to the others in the list. Ask yourself, "If I had to choose between this Exercise and Singing, which would I choose?" Mark the answer and then ask the same question with Exercise and Dancing. Go through the list comparing Exercise to each one.

Do this with each passion on your list.

Another Slice of Pi

Which passion stood above the others as the thing you would always choose?

That's the passion to focus on. That's the passion that ignites you and breathes life into your dreams. That's the passion that sings greatness into your soul. That's the passion that will help you become the Miracle in your life and a Miracle in the lives of others!

And the best part is this. Now that you know which passion moves you more than anything else, you will *Do It!*

Part 1: Transformations

Thoughts on Happiness, Growth, & Failure

Happiness is our Natural State of Being.

Unhappiness takes a lot of work. You have to focus on everything "you don't like", on everything that's "going wrong" to maintain it.

Isn't it easier to think of the blessings in your life and feel happiness and gratitude?

No matter how much we've grown, There is Always Room for Improvement.

The question is; when you stumble, do your curse the stone you tripped over, or thank it for opening your eyes to a blind spot in your vision?

Make today a great day!
Choose to learn and grow!
Choose happiness and joy!

The Only True Failure is Quitting.

As long as you keep getting up, as long as you learn from your failures and persevere, you'll never suffer defeat!

Another Slice of Pi

What does, "Be The Miracle in Your Life" Mean?

To be the Miracle in Your Life you must recognize that every choice you make, every action you take, every thought you entertain has consequences. Some of these consequences are good and others are undesirable.

Once you understand that your choices shape your life and impact the lives of those around you, you will start making better choices.

More and more, as you make better choices, you create Miracles in Your life and in the Lives of others.

So Being the Miracle in Your Life means accepting accountability for your life, for the fruits of your choices, and it means waking up and choosing a better tomorrow for you and those around you.

So I challenge you to ask yourself, "What life will I have tomorrow if I continue making the same choices I did in the past?"

The ask, "Is that the life I want?"

If it is, Great!

If it's not, then isn't it time to make better choices?

Are you ready to stand tall, accept accountability and start making better choices? Are you ready to Be the Miracle in Your Life? Are you ready to Be the Miracle in the lives of others?

Then congratulation! You're well on the way to creating the life of your dreams!

Part 1: Transformations

How Do You Handle Failure?

I have a simple question for you.

What do you do when you get knocked down?

Do you sit there and bemoan your fate?

Or...

Do you get back up, figure out what you're doing wrong and try again?

Success is a process of trying, failing, learning, trying, failing, learning. The trick is that with each attempt you learn more and get better. Just focus on the things that are going right and learn from the things that didn't.

Before you know it you'll look back and think, "Why did I ever think that was hard?"

As you step into your life today, remember you are a miracle! Now Be The Miracle! You have the power of choice! You have the ability to learn, to grow, to change!

Isn't it time you accepted how powerful you are?

Maybe that scares you. That's OK. Take a deep breath, breathe out your fear, and go conquer your day!

What is "Your Blueprint, Life by Design"?

YOUR BLUEPRINT, LIFE BY DESIGN came from the question, "What if I could use the Law of Attraction to be the ideal me?"

As I explored this, I discovered the power of the Subconscious Mind and realized that was THE KEY TO EFFECTIVELY HARNESSING THE POWER OF THE LAW OF ATTRACTION.

Up to 90% of our thoughts are Subconscious. I'm sure you've heard the phrase, "What you think about, you bring about." The Law of Attraction gives you what you think about. It doesn't matter if 10% of your conscious thoughts are about money or success or fitness or happiness if your Subconscious Thoughts, the prevailing 90%, are about lack or failure or being unhealthy or are filled with sadness!

But once you change your Subconscious Thoughts to match your Conscious Desires... That's when you Tap the Awsome Power of the Law of Attraction! That's when you're on the way to the life of your dreams!

YOUR BLUEPRINT, LIFE BY DESIGN gives clear, easy to follow directions that show you how to change any part of your life. It helps you discover who you really are and guides you on your personal path of discovery and change. YOUR BLUEPRINT, LIFE BY DESIGN, is the definitive success guidebook about using the Law of Attraction and your Subconscious Mind to create the life you desire.

Part 1: Transformations

Best of all, as you Read YOUR BLUEPRINT, LIFE BY DESIGN, you feel like you and I are having a relaxed conversation. We're two friends, sitting comfortably, discussing knowledge I've gained through my life challenges and the system I developed that's changed my life AND helped so many others redesign theirs.

If you're serious about learning to use your Subconscious Mind Power and The Law of Attraction to Be your Ideal You, then buy your copy of YOUR BLUEPRINT, LIFE BY DESIGN today!

And when you Buy your Copy of YOUR BLUEPRINT, LIFE BY DESIGN from my website http://www.YourNewBlueprint.com/ I'll personally sign it!

Remember, there's no time like Now to take control of your life. TAKE BACK YOUR LIFE! You have the power within to Be a Better You. You have the power within to Create the Life of Your Dreams. You have the power to Be The Miracle and create lasting change in your life AND the lives of those you care about. Your Subconscious Mind holds this Power, it's the key to your success! Read Your Blueprint, Life by Design and discover the Keys to Unlock the Ideal You!

Are You Pulling on The Rope?

Are you playing Tug of War with those you love?

Imagine you're standing across from someone in a grassy field. The sun is warm on your face and a soft breeze ruffles your clothing. On the ground, a thick rope stretches out between you and the other person. You both reach down and pick it up.

Then you start pulling.

The person across from you resists.

Soon you're straining with all your might. But you never gain more than an inch or two. It seems pointless. But for some reason you feel like you have to continue fighting against the person you've now labeled "Foe".

Then your muscles give out. The rope slips from your grasp. You and your opponent both fall backwards. But you notice something. The resistance is gone. You feel light and giddy. The rope is still there but now you have no desire to grasp it. You are content to lie there experiencing the deep relaxation and peace that overcomes you now that all resistance is gone.

Why do we feel that we must meet resistance with resistance? Why do we feel that we have to pull on the rope? Just because it's there?

Imagine the rope represents a conflict between you and someone you care about.

Do you have to pick up the rope when you notice it?

Part 1: Transformations

What happens in your life, and relationship with that person, when you notice the rope and choose to leave it alone?

The rope represents conflict. Conflict only occurs when you choose to resist something. Yes sometimes conflict can be helpful if you use it to grow—by focusing on what you can learn from it instead of how you can win. But mostly conflict just adds unnecessary drama to our lives.

So what do you do when you notice conflict brewing between you and someone you care about?

You can choose to grab it, to latch on, to start a Tug of War match...

Or, and I prefer this option, you can choose to leave it alone and look for a calm resolution. If you refuse to pick up the rope the other person might stomp around for awhile, but they'll usually calm down a lot quicker than if you decide to "Fight Back". Once they've calmed down you can seek a rational resolution.

Sometimes the other person might not realize the rope is there until you pick it up and give it a tug. They might do something that upsets you. But they didn't mean it the way you thought they did. That means you're choosing to be upset because you misunderstood their actions.

Seems like a silly reason to fight to me. But many, many arguments start that way!

Remember, your perception of an event often creates more trauma than the actual event!

So the next time you feel like getting into a tug-o-war with someone you care about, take a moment and ask yourself, "Do I really want to pick up this rope?"

Do you?

When you notice the rope lying there and choose to leave it alone, you're on your way to becoming the Miracle in Your life and the Miracle in the lives of those you love!

To learn more about how your perception influences your life, conflict resolution, and how you can Be the Miracle you've been waiting for, *Read "Your Blueprint, Life by Design" and "Break Your Mold: The Art of Overcoming Patterns and Behaviors That Hold You Back"*.

http://www.rolandbyrd.co/books-by-roland-byrd/

Part 1: Transformations

Excerpt from "Your Blueprint, Life by Design". *Perception is Personal Reality*

Everything is neutral until you give it meaning. And everything that happens contains equal amounts of positive and negative. Much, if not all, of the meaning you give things comes from the part of the situation you focus on. Do you focus on how the situation can help you or how it can harm you? That largely determines the impact, and meaning, of the situation for you.

Epictetus said, *"Men are disturbed, not by the things that happen, but by their opinion of the things that happen."*

Think about this: Have you ever seen a community, church, or country come together to help others after a natural disaster? Or a nation step in and defend a weaker country from an aggressor? What about situations like the civil war and massacre in Rwanda where no one really stepped in but massive, positive impact has touched the world in the years following the atrocity? The more catastrophic or horrible a situation, the more *good can come from it.* The key is that in situations like these, people have to be willing to look for the good to find it.

In Chinese cosmology Yin and Yang represent two opposite but equal forces in nature that combine to produce all that comes to be. Yin is the feminine, passive principle and is

Another Slice of Pi

exhibited in darkness, cold, or wetness. Yang is the masculine active principle and is exhibited in light, heat, or dryness. Neither Yin nor Yang is good or bad, those are meanings we apply to them. One cannot exist without the other; and nothing exists that isn't an equal combination of the two. As long as something exists, there are two halves to it.

Think of it mathematically, any number greater than zero can always be divided by two and give you a result that is greater than zero. You can also divide any positive number by two infinitely without ever reaching zero. So, as you realize, everything has two parts, two halves to it. Which half are you going to focus on, the half that helps you or the half that hinders you?

It's up to you. But I know what I choose!

So...how do you view the world?

What meaning do you give the everyday things that happen in your life? Are you optimistic and positive in most things? If so great! If you're not, that's ok too. Either way you've just made the choice to notice how you're filtering things. Not only is this the first step in changing or improving your process—because you won't change something if you don't know it's a problem—but it's a huge step toward growing into the person you want to be.

I hope you enjoyed this excerpt from *Your Blueprint, Life by Design*. *Your Blueprint, Life by Design* is available through my website http://www.YourNewBlueprint.com/, on Amazon.com and to order from all major booksellers.

Part 1: Transformations

Making Mistakes

Mistake is just another word for Failure.

And Heaven knows I've made my fair share of mistakes. I've had my fair share of failures. But I'm OK with that because I know a secret.

It's not your mistakes, it's what you do with your mistakes that defines you.

I know it can be a challenge to let go of things we've done wrong. But holding on to mistakes doesn't help anyone. True, all mistakes carry a price. Some of them only require a small token to recover from while others are life-altering-with lingering repercussions that never seem to end. But either way, all mistakes carry within lessons to help you grow into your ideal you.

The questions is, "Are you listening?"

Past is past. Nothing you do will ever change it! But the future, the Now, those are unwritten!

You are an artist. Your life, the canvas of your dreams painted with the brush strokes of your actions.

If you're haunted by anything from your past, I challenge you to ask yourself, "What can I learn from this that will help me grow and become a better person?" Then use the knowledge from your past mistakes as gifts to guide you on your road to a better tomorrow.

We all have the power to create the life we desire. We all have the power to master our destiny and succeed at life!

Some of us are afraid of that power. So we deny it and blame others for the state of our lives. But as long as we blame others, we'll never succeed.

Stop punishing yourself for your past. Start using it as a classroom to guide you to your new, bright future. Make the decision today to evolve into your ideal you. Be a miracle in your life and in the lives of others!

Part 1: Transformations

Crazy Like a Ninja!

There are lots of cool things in life that can help you grow. Some of these things might be uncomfortable.

And you know that uncomfortable really means "Scary". Many people choose their way out of anything scary. That means they're choosing their way out of exciting and possibly life changing activities!

Does that sound like you? Are you the person who really wants to do something...but opts out at the last minute—or even sooner—because it's uncomfortable?

I used to be that person!

Then I learned to ask myself this, "Do I really want to miss out because it's scary?"

I found the answer was "NO!" I want to do things that scare me. I want to have fun! I want to grow!

I'm not talking about stupid, dangerous things like driving 100 miles an hour on the shoulder of the highway during rush-hour. I'm certain that, though it would be scary, and potentially life changing—or ending—there isn't much in the way of a growth involved in something like that.

I'm talking about things like performing on stage, doing a radio interview, or learning how to dance, things that are healthy and expand the boundaries of your comfort zone.

I'm sure you have your own list of things that scare you but are still healthy growth opportunities.

So what does all this have to do with Ninjas?

One day my phone rang.

"Hello?" I answered.

"Hey sir..." My martial arts instructor said "we need one more person to be a ninja for a video shoot next week. Can you help us out?"

I thought about it for a moment. I've always wanted to be on screen, especially doing a "Karate Flick". But the thought of actually performing in front of a camera had me cold. After all, the last time I was on the hook to perform my martial arts skills was in a tournament and I'd locked up like a boa constrictor was wrapped around me.

But still this was an opportunity I'd wanted all my life... So I asked myself, "Am I going to cheat myself out of this opportunity because I'm a little scared?"

"I'm in." I said before I could talk myself out of it, got the info I needed, and said goodbye.

And you know what?

The shoot was a blast! I got to hang out with fun people and perform cool stunts! One of the best things is that I stretched my comfort zone too.

So remember that growth opportunities can be fun and rewarding too. I encourage you to say, "Yes!" the next time you're asked to do something that is healthy and a little bit scary. You'll learn and grow. You'll stretch your comfort zone. You might even have...FUN!

Maybe you can be crazy like a Ninja too. ;-)

Part 1: Transformations

Resistance Happens. What Do You Do With It?

In times of resistance True Champions are made.

It's easy to move ahead when everything is going your way. But when things get tough...when your character and mettle are tested to their limits...when you hit resistance...

What do you do then?

Do you pack it up, hang your head and quit? Or do *you persevere*?

Perseverance is the lifeblood of champions!

Take that next step when all seems lost! Then take another! And Another!

Get back up every time you fall!

Figure out what you're doing wrong and change it!

No matter what, at all costs, push through the times of pain, of doubt, of failure. Push through and move ahead. A step is a step. Every step counts! Keep moving!

Live! Learn! Grow! Never Surrender!

That's a true success mentality!

Sometimes I'm Scared

Sometimes I'm scared. I see something new or unexpected and get kinda freaked out.

Does that ever happen to you?

I used to run from situations like that.

Now I take a deep breath and move forward. I might still have that initial knee-jerk reaction--still working on moving past that--but I've learned to face my fears, to embrace them, to use them as growth opportunities.

Discomfort is a part of life. It's the subconscious mind trying to keep us inline. But what if "inline" isn't working? What if the Status Quo isn't cutting it?

Then it's time to figure out a better way! And that only happens by forging through the discomfort and training your subconscious mind to accept the unknown, the strange, the scary as exciting opportunities to grow.

I hallucinate that all of us are imperfect and have made mistakes. I know I am and have. I also know that we each have vast, untapped potential.

Isn't it time we opened ourselves to the beauty and power within? Every one of us is capable of amazing feats!

So let's wake up and make the choices necessary to create a better tomorrow for us and for everyone we interact with. Let's face the fear, move through the pain, and learn to ask better questions!

Part 1: Transformations

Every failure has the seeds of growth! Every tragedy has the seeds for triumph!

All we have to do is find them!

I challenge you to start today.

There is Beauty in Everything!

Perception

It's winter and I'm sitting in my car watching low black clouds roll in. They are haloed by lighter clouds and a few drops of sunlight.

Some would see these clouds and think how horrible it is to have cold, snowy weather or wet weather. Some see them and find joy in the expectation of a ski holiday. Some are indifferent.

I see beauty in them.

There is beauty in everything. Every breath, every beat of your heart, every moment in life is beautiful. Even things that bring us pain are beautiful. We must be willing to look for the beauty to see it though.

One thing that helps me find the beauty in everything is the knowledge that each day is a gift. Every day is a chance to learn and grow and love one more time. So take hold of today! Live it!

Discover the beauty in your life!

Part 1: Transformations

It Just Isn't Right!

Have you ever fussed over the fine details of something that just wasn't coming out right?

When I was a child I loved to draw. But I had this illusion that everything I drew should have crystalline detail. The kind of detail you see in high resolution photographs. So I'd fuss over every... single... detail... as I drew. If a line wasn't right, I'd erase it and try again, and again. Sometimes it took me hours to draw a chin or eyes. And I never thought I got it right!

As you imagine, this was frustrating. I never created art that looked remotely like what I envisioned. And the way I drew was a slow, monotonous process because I expected each part of the picture to be perfect immediately. And they weren't.

In time I stopped drawing because it was easier to just avoid it than to produce sub-standard work—at least that's what I'd convinced myself because my subconscious mind believed that anything I did had to be perfect. And that anything I couldn't do perfectly wasn't worth doing.

I also carried this pattern of behavior into the rest of my life. When I wrote, each sentence had to be perfect. I'd fuss for hours over a single sentence, trying to get all of the words in the right places and the feeling right. And, yes, writing that was slow and painful too.

What I failed to understand was that nothing is perfect. Even the most brilliant piece of art or the most celebrated work

Another Slice of Pi

of fiction has flaws in it. You and I might not see those flaws, but if you ask the artist of author they'll tell you there was something about it that wasn't exactly how they'd planned.

I also didn't realize that it takes time—and usually lots of it—to become skilled in any craft. When we listen to the Piano Virtuoso in concert what we're actually hearing is the result of thousands of hours of practice. The same is true when we watch the pro Football Quarterback throw the 50 yard touchdown. That pass is the result of a lifetime of practice.

So, as you're learning your craft, give yourself a few gifts that will help you master it.

First: Allow yourself to be imperfect. Do things the best you can and seek improvement each time. Learn from your mistakes and focus on the weak areas. In time you'll amaze others with your skill.

Second: Give yourself time to perfect your craft. Understand that it takes time and effort to hone your skills. When you understand this concept you'll find practice easier because you know that each practice adds a layer of skill to your craft. You're getting better each day!

No matter what you love, do it! Approach it with passion and enjoy the process! In time others will see your work and think, "Wow! I wish I could do that!"

And you'll know that what they see as perfection in you in really imperfect. But that it's your best and that's good enough!

P.S. Today I apply these concepts to my writing and the rest of my life. The results have been my books and this blog. they aren't prefect, but they're pretty darn good! And they are my best and that's good enough!

Part 1: Transformations

Is it Time to Retrain Your Brain?

"There are only two ways to live your life: one is as if everything is a miracle, the other is as though nothing is a miracle."
–Albert Einstein

Which path do you choose?

When you understand that everything in life is a Miracle, gratitude naturally follows. As you know, gratitude is the first step toward abundance in all areas of your life. The Law of Attraction also tells us that "like attracts like". We get more of what we focus on. When we live in a state of gratitude, we're focusing on things we're grateful for. It naturally follows that we attract more of the things we're grateful for!

"But what if I'm not grateful for something that's happening in my life?"

That's a good question.

Perhaps you have a car that doesn't run well, or that's ugly, or that uses too much gas. How do you feel gratitude about that?

The first step is to think of the good things about your car. C'mon, you know it has a few good points! Let's start with the fact that *you have a car*. Isn't that something to feel grateful for? You could be walking or riding the bus after all! And there's something else to feel grateful for, you are able to drive where you want to go!

Another Slice of Pi

You'll discover, as you focus on the good things about your life, that you get more good things in your life! It's a positive-reinforcement loop!

Focus on the good things. Get more good things!

This might take some practice. You have to retrain your brain. That might sound daunting, but it's actually easy. The trick is to redirect your thoughts when you notice you're thinking about things "you don't like" or things "you don't want". Thought Redirection simply means start thinking about something different.

For example, if you discover you're thinking, "I hate paying so much for gas!" immediately change that thought to, "I'm so glad I was able to put gas in my car!" Or, better yet, "I'm so grateful I have a car to drive!"

As you do this more and more, you'll start reprogramming your Subconscious Mind too. And that's when the real changes happen!

Perhaps this sounds silly to you. That's ok. You might choose to give it a try anyway.

After all, what have you got to lose?

Part 1: Transformations

Are You Holding On To Something From Your Past?

When I was in high school I wanted to be a great dancer.

When no one was home I'd turn up the music and just move. Jumping, spinning, and doing all sorts of crazy things. I'd never had any training. I understood nothing about dance theory. I just loved how it felt to move to music!

But I was a closet dancer. I wasn't confident in my dancing and had a fragile self-image. I was afraid what others would think if they saw me dancing. So the only time I really danced was when no one was watching. When I danced around others I used the safe, small shuffle step perfected by so many over the years.

One day I was at a formal dance with a girl I *really* liked. We were dancing and having a good time. In an effort to feel better about my dancing ability I pointed to another guy and laughed, "At least I dance better than him!"

My date looked at me and said, "No you don't!" and shook her head.

That was one of the last times I ever danced. And I think that was the last time I danced for real.

Why?

I internalized her comment. I put so much value on her opinion of my dancing skills that my subconscious mind latched onto her comment and used it as evidence to validate my fears about dancing. I'd been holding on to her opinion and letting it dictate my desire and ability to dance. From then on, every time I thought of dancing a little voice said, "remember when..." effectively squashing my desire to dance.

But you know what?

Even after all this time, there's still a part of me that wants to dance!

I've learned to let go of a lot in life. Like all humans, I'm a layered being. Over the past four years I've stripped away many layers of false notions, flawed beliefs, thinking problems, and baggage accumulated through my life. I'm still at it too! We evolve psychologically and spiritually until we die—and I believe that even when our physical bodies shed their last breath our journey continues.

Well, as I write this today I've discovered the next layer of fear and discomfort I must peel away from my subconscious. I don't know about you...

But for me, It's Time to Dance!

Part 1: Transformations

Are You Too Set in Your Ways to Change?

I hear a lot of people say things like, "I'm too set in my ways to change." or, "I'm too old to exercise." or, "That's just the way it is."

Really?

Saying you're too set in your ways to change really means; "I'm subconsciously comfortable with my life and I'm scared to change."

It's never too late to change. It's never too late to learn something new or develop a new skill or learn better behavior patterns. It's never too late to discover your true potential and become your best self!

I'm speaking from experience. I know what it's like to feel you'll never change. For most of my life I lived that way. I believed I was broken and that nothing could fix me. What I didn't know was that staying stuck in my old belief patterns was a choice. Just like buying into the lie that my history defined my future was a choice.

Once I discovered I could choose to be a different person my life underwent a miraculous transformation. I changed. I started becoming the man I always knew I could be. Depression vanished; hope shone like a searchlight in my mind and ignited the fires of creativity, self-belief, passion, and purpose!

Another Slice of Pi

What about you? Are you content to maintain the status-quo? Or are you ready to make a difference, to change the path of your future?

The first step to changing your life's path is to decide you want something better. Once you make that decision you might feel discomfort or hear voices saying, "It's really not that bad. Let's not be hasty and do something drastic." or something similar.

That's fear of change talking. It's your comfort zone resisting growth. And most importantly, it means you're on the right path! Change of any kind is uncomfortable for most people. Embrace that feeling. Let discomfort act as a way-post telling you you're growing.

So say, "Enough is enough!" Demand a better future for yourself and those you love.

Now, create that future!

Today is the perfect day to start!

Part 1: Transformations

What Do You Do When You Feel Sorry for Yourself?

Have you ever felt sorry for yourself?

It's OK to admit it. I've felt sorry for myself in the past. Most people have jumped onboard the self-pity train at least once or twice. The trick is; what do you do when you realize you're feeling sorry for yourself?

Do you wallow and look for reason to feel even worse?

Or...

Do you figure out the root cause and seek solutions?

Wallowing in self-pity is a great way to start a downward spiral. It kills motivation, zaps energy, and opens the flood gates of depression. Feeling sorry for yourself reinforces subconscious beliefs about failure and low self-worth. In fact, if you have low self-esteem your subconscious mind is always looking for things to feel bad about. That way it can say, "See! I told you so!"

But do you think feeling sorry for yourself solves anything? Does it empower you to grow or conquer your fears?

Heck No!

Sometimes you just have to tell your subconscious mind to "SHUT UP!"

You want to do this as kindly as possible though. So instead of yelling at your subconscious when that cancerous feeling of self-pity sneaks up on you, redirect your thoughts to something positive. The best way I've found is to use Gratitude. Gratitude is your immunization against despair and self-pity. Gratitude is the best antibiotic ever invented for zapping those pesky self-defeating feelings that occasionally visit each of us.

"So, how do I use gratitude to beat self-pity?"

Great question!

One way is to remind yourself that it could be worse. Say you're living out of your car—and yes I've done that—and you're feeling sorry that you don't have an apartment or house. A way to feel gratitude is to say, "I'm glad I'm able to sleep in a car instead of on the street!"

Here's another example. Maybe you're having trouble paying your bills and you're feeling sorry for yourself that you aren't bringing in the money you want. You can say, "I'm so glad I have a job!"

In both of those situations, the next step is to do something about it. Look for an apartment or a job. Feel gratitude about what you have *and* move your feet to make things better.

It may not feel like it at the time, but every situation has something good in it. There is always a lesson to learn or a path opened or something wonderful that can happen as a result of what you're going through!

Gratitude is the key to discovering these.

So the next time you're feeling sorry for yourself, take two doses of gratitude. You'll feel better right away.

Part 1: Transformations

Sometimes Crappy Things Happen! But what do you do with them?

Much of what goes on in life is outside our control. You might get hurt physically. Someone might treat you in a mean or spiteful way. But there's no way to control others. Not really. You can influence others but not control them. So there's no way to stop others from doing things that you might find hurtful. But no matter what happens, you always have free will. That means you always have the choice how you respond to the crappy things that might happen.

And there's always a lesson to learn in everything that happens. Two people could be in the same disaster. They could both lose family members. They could both suffer crippling injuries. Yet one of them will walk away a stronger person who helps others, while the other lives the remainder of their life in self-inflicted misery.

What's the difference?

Their attitude and perception of what happened, that's the difference.

I know because I've lived on both sides of the equation. I spent the majority of my life bemoaning some crappy things that happened to me as a child, things that no person should ever go through. But that a lot of people do. It wasn't until four years ago that I started learning I had control over my reactions. That was when I discovered that I could take any situation—self-imposed, caused by others, or totally random—

Another Slice of Pi

and use it for my good. And that simple change in the way I approach life has allowed me to walk through things that would have leveled me emotionally in the past. It's helped me become a resilient person who always gets back up and gets moving forward again.

You can do this too.

The secret is to approach life as a classroom. Understand that every day is a lesson. If you do something and the results are different than you'd hoped, then figure out what you must do differently and try again.

If someone does something that you feel hurt or angry about, take a step back and ask yourself, "What can I learn from this?", "What is happening in their life that they feel compelled to treat me thus?", and "How can I use this to become a better person?"

If something totally random happens that seems unfair or that hurts you, you can ask similar questions like, "How is this for my good?" or "Can I use this event to help others?"

Simply learning to reframe events can drastically alter the course of your life. It changes you from the victim of your life to the Hero of your future. And when you're the Hero of your future, you can help others too. You can become a miracle in the lives of others.

That's hard to do as a victim. Victims are too busy trying to keep themselves from drowning to help others.

So you've got a choice to make. Are you a victim? Or are you a Hero?

Either way...

You Are The Master of Your Destiny!

Part 1: Transformations

Do You Ever Jump to Conclusions?

I came home the other day to a huge pile of clothes in the middle of the living room. My first thought was, "What a Mess!"

That was quickly followed by, "I wish the kids would pick up after themselves."

Then my 4 year old daughter came running into the room and said, "Do you want to see what's under the pile, Daddy?"

Now I could have told her that we needed to do better at keeping the house clean or that there was no excuse for making a mess in the middle of the living room. But I didn't. Instead I calmed my inner neat freak and said, "Sure! Please show me!"

She started happily ripping the pile apart; throwing clothes this way and that. The mess wasn't just in the center of the room now. It covered the whole floor!

Still, I kept my mouth shut and waited while she dismantled the pile.

Then she stood back. With a huge smile and a flourish pointed to a children's game, Break the Ice, that she'd revealed.

"That's great, honey!" I said and then gave her a hug.

My daughter skipped away singing. Then my wife came up and whispered to me, "Thank you. She worked very hard to hide the game and was proud of it."

Another Slice of Pi

As you know, this could have gone quite differently. I could have immediately disciplined my daughter for making a mess. I could have cleaned it up without taking the time to understand what the mess was. But that would have been crushing my daughter's creativity. And what message would that give her about the reward that comes from working so hard if her efforts are rewarded with scolding or indifference?

You know what, she helped clean it up later and had fun doing it because she'd been able to share her project with me first.

How many times do we jump to conclusions about things and inadvertently hurt others?

I've done it. I'm sure you have too. But I'm learning. Often, it's best to stop a moment and figure out what's really going on before making a decision. When you do that you're making a rational decision based on facts instead of an emotional decision based on circumstances. Rational decisions based on facts allow you to shape your life and treat others with kindness.

If you already do this that's Great! If you're still learning, like me, I challenge you to take a breath and figure out what's really going on—or what really happened—before you make decisions.

Part 1: Transformations

Are You Giving Up On Your Dreams Because of Fear?

I'm scared of failing at My Dream.

Have you ever felt that way?

I have a good friend who has a dream. He's had this dream for years. Every year he says, "It's time to make it happen!" Then something comes up, time, money, stress... Some rational reason he shouldn't take action on his dream appears. So he puts his dream to bed for another year.

Has that ever happened to you?

There's something you want to do, something grand, magnificent, even awe inspiring? Or perhaps it's something simple. A dream that matters to you alone, that the rest of the world might not notice if it remains undone.

But for some reason you never take action on your dream!

Sure, you might start. But you never finish.

Why is that?

Fear.

Often the idea of a dream is so powerful that we're afraid of losing it. That can translate into fear of taking action on your dream because of this insidious question, "What if I fail?"

Yeah? *So what if you fail?*

Who says failure means you must give up your dream? *Failing just means you get to learn and try again!*

How can I be that insensitive?

Another Slice of Pi

What's more insensitive, to coddle someone who's paralyzed by fear of failure or to encourage them to take action and learn from their mistakes?

Yeah, to coddle them!

Take a moment and examine your life. Are you letting your dreams slide past like a forest blurring past a car's window, glimpsing them clearly for a mere second before they vanish behind you?

If you are, then have heart because you can choose to take action on your dreams! Through taking action you'll grow, you'll learn, and in time you'll succeed where others only wish to succeed.

So ask yourself right now, "What small step can I take today to create my dream?"

Now *Go Do It!*

Tomorrow, ask yourself the same question. And Then Do It!

That's your prescription for success!

Now GO DO IT!

Part 1: Transformations

Do You Know How Beautiful You Are?

You have a gift, something only you can do. Others may have similar gifts, but none can do exactly what you do exactly how you do it. It's your style, your flair, your brilliance.

But do you know what your gift is?

Have you explored the possibilities within you?

Sadly, many will answer, "No."

But you can answer, "Yes!"

It's always the right time to step into the beauty of your creation.

How?

First: Learn to love yourself. I'm speaking of love born of acceptance and gratitude. Appreciate yourself for who you are. If you're not the person you'd like to be, that's ok because you will grow into the person you want to be.

Second: Discover your passion. There is something you love doing, something that you love doing more than anything else. What is that? Figure it out and start doing it! Even if you think you're no good at it. Do It! You'll get better each time and soon you'll look back and wonder what you were afraid of.

Third: Use your gifts to make a difference in the world. Contribution is a powerful method of discovering your true potential. Often your subconscious mind will shatter the bounds of mediocrity when seeking ways to better the lives of others.

Finally: Treat yourself and others with loving kindness. If you feel animosity towards another, accept the feeling and then dissolve it using the Ho'oponopono meditation, which is repeating to yourself—toward the person, "I love you. I'm sorry. Please forgive me."

So if the person you're feeling animosity towards is named Sally—a made up name for me—then say, "Sally, I love you. I'm sorry. Please forgive me."

Repeat the Ho'oponopono meditation for five to ten minutes and every time you feel negative emotions toward the person in question. This helps dissolve the negative feelings within you and creates a bridge to healing.

You can also use this meditation to heal unhealthy emotions you might feel about yourself. Just insert your name.

Part 1: Transformations

Are You True to Yourself? Or Are You a Chameleon?

So many people try to be everything they think others want them to be.

This never works. It only leads to heartache and confusion because they're denying who they are to please others.

Isn't it better to be the best you possible! *After all, that's who you are!* **You!**

You are the perfect version of you. No one else can match your unique nature. No one else can match the combination of thoughts, feelings, experiences, and talents that make you, You!

So be You already!

Stop lying by forcing yourself into a mold others made for you.

If you're unhappy with who you are today, Then Change!
That's in your power!

You have the gift of choice. Use it to evolve, use it to shatter the chains of conventional thinking and break the bonds on mediocrity. Use your power of choice to become your best version of you!

If you're unsure where to begin, simply ask yourself, "How would the person I want to be act?"

Now start acting that way!

Every time you behave in a way that runs counter to who you want to be, just ask, "How would the perfect me behave right now?" Do this consistently and your subconscious mind will start gently shaping you into the best version of you possible. And the best thing about this method is you remain true to yourself as you grow!

Part 1: Transformations

Are You There When Others Need You?

Sometimes just Being There is the most important thing of all!

I was fixing my Grandma's Bathroom sink the other day...

It was one of those little, quick jobs that turned into a two day process. The drain was leaking and one of my cousins had tried to fix it but found himself in over his head. So when we came to visit I offered to finish the project.

The pipe fittings were welded together, the valves stuck open because of accumulated sediment, and I had to cut the old valves off with a hack saw and then chisel the pipes free from the old connections.

In the end I replaced everything but the pipes in the wall and the sink itself. It was a big job. But I was glad to do it.

My Grandma kept apologizing to me while I was working—because she felt bad that it was such a task. But there was no need to apologize because I was happy to help out. I kept telling her that. Besides, even if I wasn't happy to help, I volunteered to do it and am adult enough to accept accountability for my choices.

At one point—when Grandma was apologizing—I said, "Grandma, this is the least I can do for you after all you've done for me in my life."

She was quiet for a second and said, "All I've ever done is be here."

Another Slice of Pi

I stopped, looked up, and said, *"Grandma, sometimes just being there is the most important thing of all."*

That got me thinking.

How often are we there for those in our lives who need us?

Often, just knowing someone cares about us is a powerful healing balm. Shouldn't we return the favor? Shouldn't we pay that kindness forward?

Take a moment and ask yourself, "Am I there for the people in my life?"

I know I can do better in this area. Maybe you can too.

Let's all reach out and let others know how much we care. Let's be there for someone!

Part 1: Transformations

How Powerful is Your Subconscious Mind?

Do you know how powerful your Subconscious Mind is?

Here's a hint, if you thought something along the lines of, "I don't care." Or "Yes, I already know." Then that's your subconscious working to discount anything you read from this point on.

Why would your unconscious mind do that? **EASY! IT'S AFRAID OF CHANGE!**

Here's a true story that demonstrates the influence your subconscious beliefs have on your actions.

The other day my wife and I attended a life changing training about resetting our subconscious financial beliefs. The information and techniques in the training were brilliant and powerful. I can honestly say I walked out of the training a completely different person than I walked in.

Naturally I want to share this training with everyone because everyone will benefit from it!

I called one of my best friends, described the event to him and explained how it might benefit him. He was stoked about how the training will help him shatter the chains of financial servitude. But his subconscious mind wasn't so excited.

How do I know his subconscious wasn't thrilled?

He told me that he had a new email address. Since I was driving I asked him to email me the new address and I'd send

Another Slice of Pi

him more information about the training. He promised to send it as soon as we got off the phone...

I waited. I checked my email. I waited some more...

Right! No email.

I called him *the next day* and said, "Weren't you sending me an email so I can get you the information?"

"I forgot." He said.

And he had. The thought of sending me that email got buried by his subconscious! In fact, between the time he promised to send the email and the time we got off the phone was about 5 seconds. **IN 5 SECONDS** he *Totally Spaced Out the Action that could start him on a new path in life!*

5 SECONDS!

That's all the time it took for his mind to bury information that made it uncomfortable! Why? Because it wants to stay comfortable! But listen up! Comfortable never leads to success!

Got it?

Yeah, that's how powerful your subconscious is. It wants you to stay the same! It wants you to live right where you are because it's a scaredy cat! If it were up to your subconscious mind you'd never change, you'd never grow, you'd how you are for the rest of your life!!!!!

Sorry for the rant. Just so you know, that time I had him send me the email while I was on the phone. Will he do anything with it? Probably not. Or he might surprise me. I hope for the latter.

Thank you for reading. I hope you have a great day.

Part 1: Transformations

An Entrepreneurial Spirit

My four year old came to me the other day with five of her child-sized hangers in her hand and said, "Daddy, do you want to buy a hanger for a dollar?"

I've told many people this over the past week and gotten many different reactions. Everything from, "How cute" to "Did you say, 'you can't sell me something I already own!'"

Here's my take.

First: She's four years old. In her mind they are her hangers. She only had hangers that came from her closet and that we use for her cloths. So she was trying to sell me something that was hers.

Second: This was her first attempt at being an entrepreneur. She wanted a dollar—or more. Instead of asking, "can I have a dollar?" she found something of value and asked me if I wanted to buy it.

Third: She wanted something and took action!

As you've probably guessed, I felt her entrepreneurial venture deserved a reward. I bought one hanger. I paid her the dollar and watched her skip away happy with her success.

But, at four years old, where did she get the idea that selling something was a way to receive money?

Let me tell you our bedtime routine.

1st we say a family prayer.

2nd we read family scriptures.

Another Slice of Pi

3rd I read a few pages from <u>The Secrets of The Millionaire Mind</u>—T. Harv Eker—and we discuss any questions the children have about the concepts in it. That might seem odd to you. But consider that children are learning and developing every day. Isn't it my duty as a father to help them develop successful financial skills and attitudes?

4th I read the children a chapter from whatever book we're enjoying as a family.

Truthfully, my four year old daughter is usually asleep by the time we get to The Secrets of The Millionaire Mind. BUT she still hears it! That's the power of the subconscious mind!

Whether you're asleep, awake, distracted, or fully engaged in what you're doing, *Your Subconscious Mind is always listening!*

Do you know what you're feeding your subconscious? *Do you know the messages you're sending to the subconscious minds of those you love?*

Many people like to say they have no control over the things they think...

GARBAGE!

You can control what you do with any thought that enters your mind! And you can control what you feed your subconscious mind! Since your subconscious creates most of your conscious thoughts, *controlling what you feed your mind shapes your thoughts.*

So pay attention to the things you're feeding your subconscious mind. Pay attention to the things you're feeding the subconscious minds of those you love. If the messages you're getting aren't in alignment with your dreams or your beliefs...

Then Change Them!

After all...It's your life. It's Your Blueprint!

Part 1: Transformations

Why You Should Forgive

Why Forgive? That's a good question. I know I've felt hurt by others' actions before. If I tallied all the times I was hurt physically, psychologically, emotionally, spiritually… The list would be very long. I'm sure it's the same for you.

But what's the point?

Does it hurt the people who hurt me when I think of the things that happened?

Does it pay them back or get even with them?

Do they even know I'm thinking about it?

To think of injustices I've received in the past is like tearing open a healed wound to see if the damage is still there.

And what of the injustices I've inflicted on others? When I've learned from them, grown from them, become a new man. Does constantly examining them make them go away?

Does it change what happened?

Can anything change the past?

Does it help people I've hurt for me to punish myself constantly for something I did in the past when I was a completely different person?

Does it help you if you punish yourself for things you did in the past, when you were a different person?

Does it help those around you?

The past overflows with lessons. When we learn the lesson and grow, it's time to let it go. Besides, it's nearly impossible to grow from something you're unwilling to release.

But let's get back to why we should forgive.

If something horrible happened to you and you continually think about it, you're forcing yourself to relive that experience over and over. If you take the same event and you discover the lessons in it, then you can release it. When you release it, you stop reliving it. *That's when you truly heal.*

Part of healing is forgiving the person who hurt you.

Understand that the person may never know you forgive them. You can tell them if you want but it's okay if you don't. Forgiveness isn't about going to that person and telling them everything is okay. Maybe it's not okay. Maybe what they did was horrible beyond compare. Maybe it was life-altering for you or your family.

You should still forgive them because forgiveness isn't about them.

Forgiveness *is about you.*

Forgiveness helps you. When you make the choice to forgive, you're choosing to release hate, fear, loathing, sadness... All the things that tear at you, that bind you in chains of misery.

Forgiveness is refusing to let painful events in your past ruin your present or your future.

What if the person who hurt you did it deliberately, with malicious intent?

"Oh no, I could never forgive them..."

Why?

Reframe it. When you choose to hold hatred and anger in your heart, it's like your allowing that person to continue hurting you. In cases like that, isn't the best 'revenge' to completely let go of what happened so their actions never hurt you again?

We've all seen the person who refuses to forgive another. Sometimes it consumes their life. They begin to define themselves by the hatred they hold for the person who hurt them. That's bad enough. The truly sad thing is that *their choice to withhold forgiveness impacts everyone in their life*. Their children, friends, family, associates, everyone they interact with feels the hatred, anger, pain that they radiate.

So what do you do? How do you start forgiving?

Understand that *their actions weren't about you*. Their actions were and are about them. For whatever reason, the person who hurt you was doing the only behavior they knew to meet some need. I like to think that if the person knew a better way of meeting their needs, they'd do that instead. Again, this in no way justifies their behavior or makes it okay. It helps you understand that what they did was a desperate attempt to meet some deep emotional need.

Ask yourself, "If I were them, why would I do that?" This also helps you understand that their behavior was about them.

Look for the lessons in the event. How could this event improve your life? That might sound strange but everything has some positive in it. When you discover how something about a painful or otherwise damaging event can improve your life, you're miles closer to releasing it, to healing.

Ho'oponopono

Ho'oponopono is a prayer or meditation that you repeat while thinking of the person who harmed you. It's worked wonders in my life. You can also use Ho'oponopono while

Another Slice of Pi

thinking of yourself. How many of us hold anger toward ourselves about some past event that we should or could have handled better?

It works best if you sit quietly, without distractions. Then think of the person who hurt you or that you hold anger toward and repeat mentally; their name *I love you. I'm Sorry. Please Forgive me.*

If the name of the person who hurt you is Rick, then you'd repeat *Rick, I love you. I'm sorry. Please forgive me.* Do this at least ten times in a row every day for a week. You'll be amazed at the difference you feel.

But why would you even think *forgive me* to the person who hurt you?

What you're really saying is forgive me for holding onto the anger, hatred, hurt... I feel over your actions. When you hold on to those things it's about you. It's about your choice to remain in pain. This helps you release those feelings and that helps you heal. Again, this is only something you say in your mind. They'll never know unless you tell them.

When you chose to use Ho'oponopono on yourself, you use your name. So when I use the method on myself I say, "Roland, I love you. I'm sorry. Please forgive me." If your name is Sue, you'd say, "Sue, I love you. I'm sorry. Please forgive me." If you resist the urge to use Ho'oponopono on yourself, *then you really must do it!*

You might feel weird or silly saying that to yourself but I challenge you to try it anyway. It heals deep wounds. It reduces self-criticism. It fosters patience. It lets you know that you care and love yourself in a healthy way.

Ultimately, the real question is, "What have you got to lose?"

Part 1: Transformations

Have You Ever Been Lost?

Lost while traveling? Lost in life?

I have. More often than I care to admit. :-)

It's no fun, not knowing where you are, sometimes not even knowing how you got there.

What about those times when you got directions and you're doing your best to follow them...And you end up lost anyway?

Have you experienced that?

Yes? No? Maybe?

Well I have. In fact it happened to me just the other day.

I was traveling to a client's that I'd never been to before. But I was proactive! I got directions from someone who'd been there often. Armed with these directions I set out for what should have been a 35 to 40 minute drive.

I drove to the second gas station (Station X we'll call it) in town. "You'll be heading west and pass Station X, it'll be on your right." Was one part of my directions. So I drove past Station X. It was on my right. I was heading West. Check.

"Then you'll follow the road toward the mountains." I followed the road past Station X and toward the mountains. Check.

"Keep going until you start losing cell phone service, you'll be going up into the mountains." I kept going until I started losing cell phone coverage and I was going up into the mountains. Check.

Another Slice of Pi

"You'll come to the top of a rise and start heading down. After that you'll see a red dumpster on your right. Turn on that road. Then follow that to the fork in the road and turn left, you'll cross some rail-road tracks and the business is just up the road on the left."

I came to the top of the rise and started back down. No red dumpster...

Hmmm, maybe it's a little farther on. After all, my directions said, "If you come to Iron Town, you've gone too far." I hadn't seen that town yet, so it must be a little farther up the road.

I drove up the next rise, a few more roads to the right, no red dumpster.

I hit the next town. But it wasn't Iron Town.

Cell service was back so I called my friend and told him I missed the road somehow.

"Well did you pass Station X on the right?"

"Yes."

"The second Station X in town?"

"Yes."

"And you followed the road into the mountains until you started losing cell service?"

"Yes. But I never saw Iron Town."

"Hmmm... We'll you must have missed that too. It's a small town. Go back. This time look for the red dumpster on your left. Then turn on the road right after it. And you'll get there."

"Okay." So I hung up, turned around and started looking for the red dumpster on my left.

Did I find it?
Nope!

Part 1: Transformations

I carefully scanned every bit of the road on the way back. Nothing. So I stopped, once I had cell signal again, and did a search for the customer. What I discovered was this:

I Was Using The Wrong Map

There were three Station Xs in town. I'd never known that. I thought the third Station X was the second. The second and third stations were identical in design. Both stations were on the right of a road that went into the mountains. Both roads traveled into areas where there was no cell phone service. In fact the directions fit perfectly for both routes *except for one tiny but critical bit*. We'd never discussed the fact that one of the roads passes Station X and then curves North while the other road continues heading West.

I got to the second Station X and followed my directions. It felt surreal how the direction matched up perfectly *again*. But the difference was this time I was in the right area. I made it to the client. Two and a half hours later than I should have. And I'll never forget where that client is located!

I also reinforced a valuable lesson.

It doesn't matter how good your directions are or how good you are at following them if you're using the wrong map. You can know where you're going. You can even follow directions perfectly. But if the directions you're using don't match what's around you, you'll never reach your destination.

This is true for navigating the physical paths in life and for traveling the spiritual and intellectual byways that enhance our existence. The difference is that following the wrong life-map can end with tragic results.

How do we know whether we're in the right area with the wrong map, in the wrong area with the right map, or in the right area with the right map?

Pay Attention to the Feedback You're Getting!

That means watch, listen, and feel your results.

Do the results match what you expect? Are the results improving your life? Are they helping others? Are they bringing you closer to the destination you had in mind? Or, like my adventure above, are you just getting more confused because some things match while others make no sense?

It also reminded me that sometimes well intentioned people fail to give us all the information we need to follow their directions. It's no fault of theirs; just that they might take something for granted that's a key bit of information for our journey.

So always pay attention to the results you're getting. If they don't reasonably match what you expect, then maybe it's time to check your map.

Part 1: Transformations

The Power of Optimism

What's The Power of Optimism?

The other day it was raining. The skies were gray and the sun, with its diffused light, seemed a memory. But as I left the house I still grabbed my sunglasses...

Later I realized my sunglasses were still on my head. I shrugged and smiled. I'm just being optimistic, I thought. And that's true. Even though the weathermen said it would rain all day, I expected sunshine before the day was through.

And you know what?

I got it!

In the afternoon the sun poked its face through the clouds and bathed the countryside in golden light. Breathtaking!

Sometimes it's easy to have gray in our lives and expect it to stay. We see the clouds and think, "Oh crap! Another cloudy day."

But when you train yourself to see the gray instead of expecting sunshine, you're going to get more gray.

I'm going to let you in on a secret.

There is always some sunshine in everything.

There is always something good or beneficial in every situation. Sometimes it's right where you can see it. And sometimes you have to look for it.

But it is always there.

When you train yourself to look for sunshine, you'll have happier days and a happier life.

You've just got to have the power of optimism on your side. ;-)

Are You a Quitter?

There Are Three Ways of Handling Failure.

The first method of dealing with failure is to Give Up when you fail. Yeah, that's right, QUIT!

This is by far the easiest path. Quitters never have to worry about learning. The can forget growing. When you quit you're experiencing the only true form of failure. Quitting is also a great path if you're stuck in a victim mentality.

Why?

Because the victim mentality allows you to place blame for the condition of your life on other things, on other people, on anything but you.

Here's the rub.

If you're going to blame other people or things for your failures then how can you ever take credit for your successes? At some point you must accept the fact that you choose what to think and do.

As far as I'm aware, science hasn't figured out how to place someone else's brain in your head. So those thoughts and actions came from you!

Guess where that puts the responsibility for your life?

Right on your shoulders!

With that understanding, is quitting really the best option? In the end you have to answer to yourself.

So perhaps this question is in order, "Am I a quitter or a fighter?"

Part 1: Transformations

The second method of approaching failure is to Keep Trying The Same Thing Over and Over and Over...without learning from your mistakes...

Many people seem stuck in this mode. It's like grabbing an electric fence time and again while thinking, "It can't shock me again because it shocked me last time..."

Guess what? *Yes It Can!*

And until you *start changing your approach* it will! The only reason this approach isn't as bad as quitting is because you might figure out someday that *you must do something different if you want different results!*

So if you're stuck in this approach...there's hope.

Actually, there's hope even if you're stuck in the quitting cycle because you are human. That means you have the power of choice. You are 100% capable of change!

The third method to handle failure is to Keep Trying, Learn From Each Failure, Adjust Your Approach and Try Again! Repeat this process until you succeed. (And even then keep improving!)

This is the natural growth and learning process. It's what children do! It's what people who haven't bought into small thinking do! It's what people who learn their way out of small thinking do!

Think about it. When you were learning to walk, did you give up the first time you fell?

Did you sit on the ground, throw up your hands and say, "I guess I'm just not a walker."

Of course not!

Why?

Because *you really wanted to walk* and *you didn't know quitting was an option!*

So why would you give up on things today just because they get a little hard?

Right! There's no good reason! So get back up, get out there, *figure out what you're doing wrong, and Change Your Approach!*

There's a word for this process...*Success!*

Part 1: Transformations

Kick The Quitter Out of Your Life!

Isn't it time you *Kicked The Quitter Out of Your Life!*

Awhile back I wrote a letter to the Quitter in my life. It was healing and had dramatic, immediate results in my life.

The idea is to write a letter to Mr. or Mrs. Quitter. Tell them why you're done with them. Dig deep. Find powerful reasons why you're through with the quitter inside.

I challenge you to write your own letter today!

To give you an idea what it looks like, here's the letter I wrote.

Dear Mr. Quitter

I remember you. You showed up early in my life. You told me I wasn't good enough, that I'd never amount to anything. Your voice changed from time to time, but the messages were the same.

"Why make friends?" You'd say, "You're just going to move again anyway."

"Why try that? You'll never win!"

"You're doing what? You Idiot! Do you really think you'll succeed? Give it up now before you embarrass yourself."

"Oh, this is hard. Let's take the day off and watch TV or play video games."

But then one day I decided to try skateboarding. I had you in a real snit! "You can't do that! You're too old! You'll get

Another Slice of Pi

hurt! People will laugh! Everyone things you're an idiot for trying this!"

The problem for you was that I Wanted To Skateboard *like I'd never wanted anything in my life.* "Shut the %^&%^! UP!" I screamed. *And I meant it.*

You didn't stop talking about skateboarding right away. It took months and months before you realized you weren't going to change my mind. When I showed you that I could skate in a skatepark during the busiest time of day, or right next to a freeway with thousands of people driving by **and love it**...that's when you stopped bothering me about skateboarding.

Then you moved to other things. But I'd beaten you once. I knew I could do it. That was the beginning of a new life for me.

I beat you when I published my first book. I beat you again when I published my second book. Every day you grow weaker and weaker in my life.

Well I have news for you. I know you've been holding on to finances as your last refuge, the place where you'll keep me down. Here's the rub.

I want financial success every bit as badly as I wanted to learn to skateboard. I think it's fair to say I want financial success more than I wanted to learn to skateboard. You know I beat you on my skateboard. You know I beat you with my writing. You know I'm beating you in my financial life too! So you'd better pack your bags. Cuz I'm kicking your lousy %$#! Out of my life for good!

Leave Now and Never Come Back!
Roland

Part 1: Transformations

Once you're done writing the letter go read it out loud in the mirror. Allow yourself to feel the emotions you expressed in your letter. Look yourself in the eye and let the inner quitter know you're serious. This is it! You're done with them for good!

After reading your letter, take immediate action on one of your dreams. This helps solidify your intention.

The next time you feel like quitting, just remember *you kicked the quitter out!* That quitter is gone for good! So tell it, "Thanks but I'm doing this anyway!"

Are You Withholding Forgiveness?

Forgiveness is often misunderstood. People withhold it for many reasons. Are any of these familiar to you?

Some withhold forgiveness because they believe forgiving validates what someone else did.

Some withhold forgiveness because they believe holding on to the injury punishes the other person.

Some withhold forgiveness because they believe their injury gives them strength.

In truth, there are countless reasons people withhold forgiveness.

All of them flawed.

In reality:

Forgiveness shatters the chains of hate.

Forgiveness heals wounds of the heart and soul.

Forgiveness restores hope, love, joy, and purpose.

Forgiveness allows you to get on with your life!

So if you're holding on to something that slowly festers in your soul, as yourself, "Why? What purpose does it serve?"

Forgiveness is a Balm for Your Heart & Soul

What are you holding onto?

Why?

Does it help you when you clutch tightly to your pain, your anger, your anguish?

Does it help those you love?

Part 1: Transformations

You know these answers.

If there's something you're holding onto, forgiveness you're withholding for a real or imagined wrong, isn't it time you let it go?

Isn't it time to *Forgive*!

Only you can release yourself from the chains forged by anger, hate, and pain because, like it or not, you forged the chains.

It might seem hard to let these things go, but in the end your life will be so much better when you're free from the anchors of your past.

Make a New Start Today!

It's Time to Get Uncomfortable!

It's easy to float along with the status-quo in life. It's easy to rationalize your way out of opportunities to grow because growth is uncomfortable.

But who are you really cheating?

It's obvious that refusing to grow kills your passion for life. If you doubt this, just look at someone who's caught in a daily grind. They rarely do anything new. They usually complain about life. They have dead eyes. There's no fire, no zest, no energy!

Do you know someone like this? Of course you do, they're everywhere!

Then look at someone who challenges themselves regularly. There's bounce in their step, life in their eyes, infectious energy radiating from them.

What's the difference?

In life we're either growing or dying. There is no standing still. I know that each day is one day less for everyone. No one lives forever. That's different. Your mind, your heart, your passion, your creativity, your spirituality, your body, the things that make life interesting and meaningful, that's what I'm talking about!

You know a surefire way to have your body fall apart is to quit using it. Look at any couch potato if you need proof. The same thing goes for your mind, your passion, your creativity and the other things listed above. If you stop challenging

Part 1: Transformations

yourself in any of those areas you atrophy. That means that part of you starts dying.

How do you fight this?

Simple! Do at least one thing new every day. You might go somewhere new, learn about a new subject, talk to a stranger, exercise, write, draw, paint, dance... The list goes on and on. If it feels uncomfortable and it's good for you then give it a shot!

The real question is, "*Who do you want to be?*"

Life happens no matter what you do. You might as well make it a wonderful life! Stretch your mind! Encourage others! Make a difference! Do something that matters! Make learning and growing a habit. Do this and you'll be amazed at the results in your life!

Another Slice of Pi

The Power of "What If?"

What if? A simple question; that's equally powerful and destructive depending on its context.

It's easy to think of the past and wonder...

What if I'd done this?
What if I'd done that?
How would things be different today?

The truth is you'll never know what might have been. Doors from the past, divergent paths are closed. Besides, wondering how your life would be today—if you'd acted differently in the past—is a good way to drive yourself mad.

But more importantly, habitually wondering "What if?" breeds depression. It kills motivation. It's like trying to run a 100 meter sprint through quicksand. When you're stuck in, "What if?" you're living in the past—punishing yourself for it.

What's that accomplish?

Everyone can look back and find things they could do differently.

When you're looking back you've got the knowledge of now with you. If reviewing a past situation reveals nothing you could have done differently, chances are you either handled it well or you haven't learned how to deal with that situation—the solution is outside your understanding.

When you look at things that spark, "What if?", do it with the intent to learn. Resist the temptation to blame or punish

Part 1: Transformations

yourself. Instead, take knowledge your new perspective gives you and use it to become a better person.

What about the powerful side of, "What if?"

Take the question and spin it on its head! Instead of asking, "what if I'd done..?" ask, "what if I do?". Apply it to the future. And open yourself to wondrous possibilities!

> *What if I write that book?*
> *What if I take that trip?*
> *What if I apply for that job?*
> *What if I climb that mountain?*
> *What if I succeed?*

Use "What if?" to ignite your imagination's fire. Use it to discover your passion. Use it to paint a brilliant future!

The choice is yours. You can punish yourself for the past or you become the hero of your future.

Do You Know The Power of Gratitude?

Thanksgiving is a wonderful holiday. One day a year set aside to fully express Gratitude for Life's Blessings.

Gratitude is a wonderful gift that we should practice every day. Gratitude not only dissolves disempowering emotions like depression, anger, frustration, & anxiety—to name a few, it opens you to receive more blessings because it places your *focus on what you have* instead of what you lack.

Sadly, many people think they must receive something to feel thankful.

But the truth is, no matter where you are in life, you can always feel grateful. *There's always something to feel gratitude for.*

Even if it's something as simple as:

"I'm thankful I have warm blankets."

"I'm grateful for the gift of another day to become a better person."

"I'm grateful for the air I breathe."

"I'm thankful for my body."

"I'm grateful for a hot meal."

In reality, Everything You Need to Experience Love, Joy, and Fulfillment is *already within you*.

Once you realize that, you'll begin to feel grateful for the gift of life. Every breath, every thought, every beat of your heart are reasons to celebrate. These mean you're alive, empowered to create your future, to make a difference should you choose.

So tap into gratitude. Think of five things right now you're grateful for. But instead of stopping there, do your best to make this a daily practice. You'll be amazed at the difference living in gratitude creates in your life.

Follow Your Heart or Follow the Herd

I woke up one morning and realized I was following the safe path. I was following the course society set for me in my career and in my life. I wasn't following my heart. I was living as the victim of my history, shackling myself with beliefs and actions other's dictated, afraid to forge through the pain of change because the pain of existing in numbness and despair was what I knew. I was following the herd.

After all, aren't we taught to be consistent? Aren't we taught to play it safe?

But ironically the safe path I followed was only safe because it was what I knew. The path I was on was fraught with anguish, anger, despair, self-loathing, and narcissism. I was so busy trying to protect myself from anything that could possibly harm me, that I'd become a loathsome creature indeed.

Then I woke up. I decided there must be a better way and that even if it killed me, I was going to find it because my family deserved better from me. Life and God deserved better from me. I made the decision that no matter what, I'd succeed. I started following my heart. And I forged ahead, and forged ahead, and forged ahead…

Waking up was a painful process. It took courage and perseverance. It taught me that I was stronger than I'd ever imagined, that I was softer than I knew, and that I could truly care for others. Waking up taught me that I could change,

Part 1: Transformations

overcome old programming, choose who I was (or perhaps awaken to who I'd always been under all the pain and madness), and become that person. Waking up was the best thing I ever did. It's the reason I'm still here. It's the reason I write this blog and write books to help others.

I started waking up almost six years. Since then I've committed myself to living every day to the best of my abilities, to learning and growing continually, and to helping others.

Are you ready to wake up?

Are You Happy?

I hope you are. After all, what is a life devoid of happiness? But sadly, many answer, "No" to this critical question.

In western society we're taught happiness comes from things or experiences or people. That's flawed because external things, people, and experiences don't *make* us happy. The truth is we allow ourselves to feel happy when our happiness rules are met.

Think about it. Two people can go through the same event and each come away with a different meaning. For example; one business owner might feel thrilled when the opportunity to land a big contract comes because it means more revenue or the chance to expand the company. Another business owner might have the same opportunity but feel annoyed that they need to fill out the bid or feel fear about the tax bracket the extra revenue will put them in.

It's the same situation. So why does each react differently?

Their happiness rules—let's call them their personal laws of happiness. The first business owner has laws of happiness that mean increased money is something to feel happy about. And the second business owner has laws of happiness that make extra money something to worry about.

What about a simpler scenario?

Think about a rollercoaster. You reach the top of the first hill. The car drops. Your stomach leaps into your chest. The

Part 1: Transformations

wind buffets your face. You scream as the car rockets through the first turn...

Is your scream one of joy or fear?

Your feelings about a rollercoaster ride are based on your personal laws of happiness and are unique. I feel differently about rollercoasters than you do. The next person who reads this will feel differently than both of us. There's no way around it.

Everyone has different rules about happiness.

But if you're unhappy there's good news. Heck, even if you're happy there's good news.

Happiness is within you! It's already there!

You choose whether you feel happy or not. You get to decide how you feel. No one can take that from you.

I know someone's gonna say, "But my life sucks! What do I have to feel happy about?"

Start with the simple things. Are you breathing? That's something to feel happy about. If you're reading this, you can see. If you're listening to this, you can hear. *You're alive!* You can think. You can make choices. You can change your happiness rules.

No matter what condition your life is in today, you have the power to change it! That's something to feel happy about.

The best part is, once you choose to feel happiness in the simple things, it blooms and you'll discover more and more happiness in your life!

Your life is a story, a grand adventure full of hope and wonder and love and happiness. *Get out there and live it!*

Break Free of Old Patterns

Have you ever wanted to break free of your past programming—of the patterns or habits that hold you back?

I know I have. I imagine you have too.

But how do you do it? HOW DO YOU BREAK FREE? Where do you even start?

After all, most of the habits and patterns that undercut our success are deeply seated in the subconscious mind. That means we're usually unaware we're running them until the subconscious script has played out. And when we are aware of them, it can feel like watching a character in a B horror movie. You see them walking right into danger, but no matter how much you scream at them to stop...

Yeah, they keep right on going.

Now that's not entirely fair. Once you're aware you're behaving from an old or unhealthy subconscious behavioral pattern, you can *stop it!*

Yes, You Can!

First, avoid the temptation to berate yourself when this happens because that won't help. Mentally punishing yourself for unwanted patterns of behavior actually reinforces them.

Why?

Because it focuses on what you want to stop doing and has powerful emotions at the same time. That's the recipe to tell your subconscious that something's important. And that's

Part 1: Transformations

the opposite of what you want when you're breaking an old pattern.

Instead, come up with something to stop your pattern, something totally unexpected. You might think of a ridiculous phrase that you'll shout if you notice yourself acting in an old pattern. It helps to plan this in advance so you're ready if you need it.

Let's use the phrase, "OOOGLY! BOOGLY! PRESTO! MISTRO!" (Yes I know it's totally ridiculous. That's the point)

Now remember a situation you could have resolved better, one where you were reacting instead of responding and where your reaction was out of proportion.

Got one?

Great!

Now remember exactly how that felt. Remember why you felt that way. Remember what you said and how you said it. Remember what you were doing with your body. Get it really clear in your mind. And now shout, "OOOGLY! BOOGLY! PRESTO! MISTRO!"

No, really, go ahead and shout it now! "OOOGLY! BOOGLY! PRESTO! MISTRO!"

Ok. If you're at work, then shout it in your mind.

Now go ahead and remember the event again. Get it really clear in your mind again. Remember how you felt and why you felt that way. Remember what you said, how you said it, and what you were doing with your body. Get it really clear in your mind again...

Now shout, "OOOGLY! BOOGLY! PRESTO! MISTRO!"

Are you laughing? Do you feel different now?

Chances are YOU SAID YES. That's because you just interrupted your old pattern of behavior.

Another Slice of Pi

You can use any phrase you want for this. Just make sure it's ridiculous and totally unrelated to what you're feeling when you use it. It helps to have a few different phrases in your mental tool kit too. So prepare a few right now—so you're ready when you need them.

Awesome!

Now that you know this technique, I challenge you to use it! Go ahead and give it a try over the next 14 days and let me know how it works for you.

Part 1: Transformations

Why Me? Is a Very Dangerous Question.

Have you ever wondered, WHY ME?

I used to wonder, WHY ME? all the time. But you know what? WHY ME? is a very dangerous question because it feeds the concept that you aren't in control of your life. And while you aren't always in control of the things that happen to you, you're always in control of how you internalize it—the meaning you give those events. And the meanings you give events in your life are the cobblestones of your future.

Yeah, I know it's easy for me to sit here and say you should avoid the question. So let me tell you a story about how I reframed an event in my life and the difference that made.

Not Today

I love motorcycles. Riding a motorcycle is like flying. Nothing compares to the wind against your skin, the changes in temperature, the scent of flowers, grass, and trees. There's no roof to block your view of the countryside, no window frames to cut a scene in half. The ability to lean deep in a corner and shoot out the other side is like surfing an asphalt wave.

I smile just thinking about it.

A little over a year ago I was riding my motorcycle. I'd just left a client's, and was heading back to the office, when it happened. I was on the on-ramp for the freeway. I was clear to the side. I checked over my shoulder and saw that there was ample room for me to merge with traffic. I looked forward again and was still clear. So I started to accelerate down the remainder of the on-ramp. I quickly checked over my shoulder again and was still clear. I looked forward... A minivan—slightly to the front and the left of me—was hard on its brakes cutting into my on-ramp lane, cutting me off.

This all happened in seconds...

I had nowhere to go. There was too much traffic on the freeway for me to shoot to the left. And I wasn't going fast enough to merge with traffic anyway. Besides, the angle the minivan was traveling put it right in my path if I tried to veer left. So in an attempt to avoid the minivan, I immediately applied the front and rear brakes and tried to angle my bike to the right and off the road. But they were breaking too hard and cutting too sharply across my lane (the on-ramp). Then I tried to lay my bike down so I could kick off and at least slide it out.

No luck.

I was in a side-ways slide leaning at about a 45° angle, a second more and I'd have been able to lay the bike down and kick off. That's when the minivan hit me, right behind the front wheel of my bike.

I thought, "Not Today!" And I thought of my wife and children and how much I love them.

I was launched off my bike like a human rocket, except I didn't have a safety net. That's right, I was airborne—at about 55mph...

Martial Arts Anyone?

Instinct, from many years of martial arts training, took over. I immediately tucked then I slammed into the ground and rolled, and rolled, and rolled... Seriously it felt like I tumbled forever! And it wasn't like on the mat at karate either.

Part 1: Transformations

This was like being stuck in an industrial-sized clothes dryer. WHAM! Thump, thump, thump, WHAM! Thump, thump, thump, WHAM!

A road-side marker finally stopped my roll somewhere between fifty and one-hundred feet up the freeway—I'm a little fuzzy on that part because my head (in a helmet thank you) hit the asphalt at least four times as I bounced along.

So I lay there with this road-side marker pressing into my lower back and I thought, "I'm glad I survived." Then I thought again of my wife and my daughters and sons, and how glad I was that I'd get to see them again. I didn't try to move because I didn't know how bad the damage was. All I knew is that I hurt everywhere—and that's a colossal understatement.

I continued to lay there while good Samaritans asked me questions. Then they helped me sit up while we waited for the ambulance. It was then, while waiting for the ambulance that I had a thought that surprised me at the time. *"I wonder what the lesson in this is and who it's for?"*

I never wondered, "Why me?" In fact that was the farthest thing from my mind.

As I sat there, I mentally reviewed the events of the accident and my day up to that point and I never felt I should have done something differently. In fact, it seemed that everything had happened in a perfect orchestration to bring it to pass. So I knew there was a reason for it. I'm not sure what the reason was. I believe it was a lesson. Maybe it was for the lady who hit me, the people who pulled over and helped, the officer who arrived and investigated the accident, my family, me, or even the paramedics who took me to the ER—and who, at my suggestion, took pictures of my helmet to show in motorcycle safety presentations. Maybe it was a lesson about what

Another Slice of Pi

you can survive if you wear your helmet and other motorcycle gear.

Truthfully, there are a lot of lessons in what happened that day. But they would have been lost on me if I'd been entrenched in, "Why Me?" That question would have led to anger and resentment. It would have placed me as the victim of the accident. And while I was physically traumatized, I would only become a victim if I believed it so.

Another nice byproduct of asking, "What lesson is in this?" instead of ,"Why Me?" is that it helped me easily forgive the woman who hit me. I could have put a lot of energy into blaming her for the accident and into feeling like she wronged me. But truthfully, I felt no anger toward her. It's not like she woke up that morning and thought, "I'm gonna get me a motorcyclist today!" In fact she was very apologetic and concerned for my well-being.

So next time something happens to you that hurts, that you feel angry about, or that's just plain out of your control, try leaving WHY ME? behind and asking better questions instead.

Questions like, "WHAT LESSONS ARE IN THIS?" And, "HOW CAN I USE THIS TO HELP OTHERS?" are a great place to start. Seek the knowledge and understanding that the experience offers you. You'll be glad you did.

Part 1: Transformations

How Emotionally Flexible Are You?

(This is an excerpt from my book on personal transformation, BREAK YOUR MOLD.)

That really comes down to this question, WHAT DO YOU DO WHEN RESISTANCE HAPPENS IN YOUR LIFE?

Many fight resistance. They might scream, convulse in anger or frustration. They might bemoan their fate or curse their luck. Often people quit, throw up their hands and say, "That's it! I'm done!" Then they walk away from their dreams.

What does that accomplish?

Right!

Nothing worthwhile.

Anything worth having, achieving, or changing takes effort. Changing how you approach life, and the results you get, takes effort! Sometimes you'll meet resistance. At others, you'll glide effortlessly through this process.

Either way, *you must persevere*. Being Emotionally Flexible allows you to do just that!

Think of your life path as a streambed. Resistance is a boulder thrown in your streambed. If you're a rock rolling through your streambed, chances are you'll roll into the boulder, get chipped or cracked and stop moving! Depending on your speed, you might even shatter.

But if you're water flowing through your stream bed, you'll meet the boulder, fill up the stream bed until you flow

Another Slice of Pi

around the obstruction, and continue on your way. Sure, the obstacle delayed you as you filled up enough to flow around the edges. But it never stopped you. It never damaged you. It *only* slowed you—while you grew enough to get around the obstacle.

Another great example of managing challenges in life is wind. Imagine you're the breeze floating across a meadow on a warm summer day. As you near the edge of the meadow you discover trees in your path. These are simple. You effortlessly glide around them and continue on your way.

They hardly slow you down.

Next you come upon a shack, sagging against the mountain side like a tired old man. You flow over its splintered wood and through empty windows. You fill its lone room with warmth and the smell of flowers before exiting the other side and flying across the mountain. The shack slows you more than the trees, but you still pass it without effort or difficulty.

But what if you're a boulder rolling through the meadow? When you hit the trees, you'll Hit The Trees! You won't make it far because the trees become a giant net, slowing you, trapping you. *And* you're going to break some trees too! Forget making it to the cabin. Every tree you hit steals your momentum. It won't take long before you're at a standstill.

Wind and water have two main things in common. They *both take the path of least resistance* and they both *keep moving!*

Wind and Water adapt to situations effortlessly and persist in their path.

A rock may try to take the path of least resistance but it's incapable of adapting. A rock will plow through or break against most things that wind and water slip around. Everything the rock hits slows it down. Sure, it might crush an obstacle, but it loses energy and momentum with each one. And, as you realize, when a rock crashes into something bigger or harder, the rock takes a lot of damage.

Is that how you want to live?

Rocks live tough lives. I know. I used to be one...

Emotionally that is.

How can the principles of adaptation and persistence make a difference?

Here's an example from my life:

The Boulder

I used to have the emotional flexibility of a boulder. I talked down to myself all the time. If something wasn't happening how I thought it should, I felt anxious and scared. Often, I'd feel angry because I couldn't stand feeling out-of-control. But I felt out-of-control any time things weren't going according to my plan.

As you know, life's rarely ordered, logical, or predictable! That means things rarely went according to my plan. The very nature of life meant that I almost always felt out-of-control. So I almost always felt angry, anxious, and scared. (You understand the problem with this pattern of thinking.) So I used to try to force order on my life anyway, to make it comfortable for me.

It was all about me... Aside from being a selfish way to live; that resulted in lots of stress and anxiety!

Why?

I was trying to control things that were outside my control. There are things you can directly impact or influence in your life. There are many, many things you aren't able to impact or control though.

Do you know the difference?

I didn't.

So I lived in a state called "Hyper Vigilance". I tried to control everything, and I mean everything, that happened in my life. This behavior wasn't just because I like order, logic, and predictability. I hadn't learned to deal with many things that happened to me as a child. Hyper Vigilance was my subconscious mind's way of trying to protect me from harm. The root subconscious belief was, IF I CAN CONTROL EVERYTHING IN MY LIFE, NOTHING CAN HURT ME.

But you know what?

That belief is fundamentally flawed because:

There's no way to control everything that happens in life because there are many other players in the game. You can't control others. Nor should you try.

You're responsible for how events impact you. No matter how crappy something is, you're the one who decides what you do with it. That means horrible, even tragic events can be used for your good—and the good of others—when you choose to use them that way.

Once I learned those concepts, life was much easier to bear. I began to love life because I understood that happiness and love are choices.

I started choosing happiness and love. I stopped being a strong, inflexible, fragile rock and started becoming like wind and water. Make no mistake; wind and water are strong too.

Part 1: Transformations

They can wear down cliff faces, topple trees, and reshape their landscape. They do that when necessary. But for the most part, they work with slow precision creating change that runs deep and lasts.

Which will you choose?

Why Do You Care What Others' Think?

Really; WHY DO YOU CARE WHAT OTHERS' THINK?

I used to worry so much about what others' thought that I was paralyzed by fear. I put off doing things I loved because I might look foolish. I rarely tried new things for the same reason. I felt like I was walking in a spotlight, like everyone was watching, judging my every word and movement.

You might imagine the havoc that creates. How can you ever learn new things or improve when you're terrified of trying because, "Someone might see me mess up…"

When I remember what it was like to live that way, I'm dumbstruck. Seriously, the energy it takes to constantly worry about what others' think is exhausting! It's hardly living. It's like I was a prisoner, shackled in the cell of my fear!

Maybe you can relate to how that feels, maybe you can't. I hope you can't honestly because life is too short to let fear of people's opinions rule you.

Here's an example of how I used to let fear of others' opinions control me:

Defeated

About 10 years ago I was working out almost every day. I'd go to the gym in the morning and exercise for two hours and then go to work. I was in great shape and I loved my time in the gym. For over a year I was a regular.

Part 1: Transformations

Then I missed a few days because of a family vacation. No big deal, right? Just get my butt back in the gym as soon as the vacation was over.

That's the logical thing to do. Is that what I did?

Not so much.

I'd only missed five days, less than a week... I got up, got my things together, and drove to the gym. But when I got there, waves of fear and anxiety washed over me. I gripped the door handle in my car. But I couldn't bring myself to open it. I wanted to, desperately. But the voices in my head were louder than my desire to workout.

I knew that my friends would think I was a fool for missing my workouts over the past few days.

I knew I'd let them down.

I knew I'd failed at my goal to get in the best shape of my life.

I knew they'd talk behind my back about my lack of dedication, that they'd point and jeer when I wasn't looking...

After about 30 minutes sitting there, I tucked tail and drove to the office, defeated.

After that it became easier to miss my workouts. I was in a self-defeating cycle. I wouldn't go to the gym because I feared others' opinions. Each day I missed at the gym strengthened my fear of what they thought. You certainly understand the problem with this pattern. Soon I'd rationalized that I didn't want to work out at the gym anyway. And because we moved before I learned to overcome my fear of what others' thought, I never set foot in that gym again. In fact, I stopped working out for a few years after that and ended up in the worst physical shape of my life, which I overcame later—but that's another story for another time.

Another Slice of Pi

I eventually overcame my fear of, *what others' thought*, and learned some valuable lessons:

People's opinions are their own. They have more to do with them than you (or me).

People are rarely watching us, judging our every action. And even if they are, *So What? Who Cares What They Think!*

You only control your actions. What other's think is outside your control. So do what you know is right because its right and let others worry about themselves.

Relax your rules about being perfect. If you miss a day, or two, or ten doing something you want to do, then just stop the slide and take action. Get back in your routine as quickly as possible. Face it, life happens. Sometimes things are going to get in the way of what you want to do. Accept that up front and it's easier to navigate through distractions and obstacles.

Every time you take action in the face of fear, the actions get easier. In time you forget that you were ever afraid.

Hopefully you've never experienced this type of fear personally. But if you have, that's okay. You can get past it.

Start by asking yourself the following question...

What would happen if I stopped being afraid of that?

Then break the thing you want to do into the smallest possible step And Do That Step Now!

Keep repeating this process and you'll soon discover your fear has vanished and you're taking action on your dreams!

Part 1: Transformations

What I Wish I'd known When I Was Younger.

As part of a meditation challenge I'm participating in I was asked to write about the things I wish I'd known when I was younger. This was a great experience for me and I wanted to share these things with you. They are lessons that have truly impacted my life.

I wish I'd known how powerful our intentions are, that we can choose our future by focusing on the good things we want to create and by having faith in the process.

I wish I'd known that we control our own lives, we may not control the events in our lives but we always have control over our interpretations of those events and how we let them shape our lives.

I wish I'd known that just because an adult, someone who 'knows', or even society at large believes something, that doesn't make it true.

I wish I'd known that what we believe about ourselves is the most powerful indicator of what will come and who we'll be.

I wish I'd known that at any moment we can shift our beliefs and alter our destiny.

I wish I'd known that we can cast off the chains of disempowering beliefs before they become prisons for our minds, hearts, and souls. And even then, we can shatter those bonds if we're willing to just wake up and do the work necessary to shake our minds free of the hypnosis that clouds them.

I wish I'd known that regardless of the things that happen to us, we are never doomed to repeat other's mistakes unless we allow ourselves to live in blindness to the truth of our existence—that we are powerful beyond measure and create our own reality.

I wish I'd known the meaning of unconditional love, that we can love someone without agreeing with their actions, and that sometimes we must love someone at a distance if their choices are harmful to our wellbeing.

I wish I'd known how to believe in myself, that I have value—we all do—and that regardless of other's opinions of me, I choose who I am and how I feel.

I wish I'd known that every dream is seeded with the ability to bring it to pass.

I wish I'd known the power of persistence, that small steps create miracles.

I wish I'd known that failure is a beautiful gift that allows us to grow and is necessary to creating mastery in anything.

I wish I'd known the power of forgiveness, that it heals our hearts and souls, and empowers us to live with the lessons of the past without being anchored in misery.

I wish I'd known that every soul has infinite worth and there is meaning in every life—even mine, even yours.

I wish I'd known that love is a choice. The first signs of love are chemical reactions designed to ensure propagation of our species. But once that wears off, then true love can blossom if we let it, if we remember the amazing things about the one we love, if we count their good points instead of bemoaning their faults, if we take the time to let them know they mat-

Part 1: Transformations

ter, if we give them attention and kindness, that's when love grows.

I wish I'd known that other's opinions only matter if we let them and that people almost always interpret our actions through their personal view of reality. Meaning that when someone thinks your actions mean something, it's because that's what those actions would mean if that person was doing them.

I wish I'd known that Love and Joy are the essential truths of our being.

I wish I'd known that we are as happy as we allow ourselves to be, that emotional pain and suffering are caused by focusing on the things that aren't how we want them to be.

I wish I'd known to count my blessings every day and to live in gratitude, that this practice makes life beautiful and adds magic to the most mundane aspects of our existence.

I wish I'd known that we can't control everything in our lives and that trying to is folly. It only creates anxiety, frustration, discontent, and despair when we clutch tightly to things that are out of our control.

I wish I'd known that well intentioned people sometimes try to crush another's dreams in misguided efforts to protect them.

I wish I'd known that our thoughts create our reality and that we never do anything without thinking of it first. No person can consistently behave one way while thinking another.

I wish I'd known that the purpose of life is to serve others and make the world a better place.

I wish I'd known that perfection is an illusion and that chasing it hinders our progression. True mastery comes only with time and doing.

Another Slice of Pi

I wish I'd known how to love myself then, but now I do. :-)

These are things I wish I'd known when I was younger. But I didn't. And that's okay. I know them now. My life unfolded and I learned these things as I was ready for them.

Your life is also unfolding in the way necessary for you to learn the things you must know to progress to your next level of awareness. So take a deep breath, go look in the mirror and say, "I love you."

Part 1: Transformations

The True Power of Gratitude

Gratitude is like a flower. When you water it, nourish it, and give it sunshine, it grows into a plant that can take your breath away with its beauty. But if you ignore the flower and don't water it or place it in a darkened room, it withers and often dies.

So what? What's it matter if you have gratitude in your life?

Have you met someone who's angry about everything? They curse their fate. They curse life. They complain about almost everything. They walk around with a frown permanently etched on their face. Even when something wonderful happens they seem to look for the *catch,* the hidden *got'cha* that will bring it tumbling down.

Yeah, I've met them too. That's a person who doesn't realize the power of gratitude, that gratitude is critical to happiness and success in life!

I'll let you in on a secret; years ago I used to be that person. But that's another story.

Gratitude is a force in your life whether you admit it or not. It's either there, working for you or it's absent and working against you. Gratitude matters because the more grateful you feel for what you already have, the more things to feel grateful for show up!

But it's more than that! Gratitude also breeds happiness, it creates hope, it fills your heart with love and casts out dark-

Another Slice of Pi

ness. Gratitude dissolves anger, it overcomes hate, it invites optimism where none was welcome before.

Gratitude is one of the most powerful forces in your life. It's an emotion that can shatter inner barriers and move you to inspired action. Gratitude is fuel for the passionate fire of your existence.

If you doubt this, consider the following.

Have you ever seen a person who's truly grateful for something? I mean have you ever really experienced their reaction? They smile, they laugh, they might even cry with joy. Their whole countenance is full of love and light.

Remember a time you felt true gratitude yourself. Remember how warm you felt. Remember how your heart overflowed with joy. Remember how you were moved, perhaps beyond words.

When you live in gratitude, you live with happiness, love, hope, and optimism. And that's a powerful way to live. Living in gratitude invites miracles into your life and allows you to be a miracle for others.

Perhaps you struggle with feeling grateful. You might think there's really nothing to feel grateful for in your life.

Instead of me telling you, "Of course you have things to feel grateful for!" Let's do a quick exercise.

Take a deep breath and release it. Now think of three things you're grateful for. If nothing comes at first, just let your mind sit and expect an answer. Once your answers come, write them down. Then make the decision to find at least three more things you're grateful for today.

And before you go to bed tonight, write down all the things you feel grateful for. It can be a short list. The power comes in making the list. The fact that *you're going to make*

Part 1: Transformations

the list helps shift you into a state of expectancy for gratitude. You're essentially telling your subconscious mind that you know there's something out there to feel grateful for and that you want it to help you find it.

When I was first learning how to feel grateful, I often had to go to the basics to find things to feel grateful about. My gratitude list would include things like *I'm grateful I'm breathing, I'm grateful I have socks, I'm grateful I have a blanket, I'm grateful I ate my last meal...*

Buy you know what?

The more I focused on what I was grateful for, the more grateful I felt. As I felt more and more grateful, more and more things to feel grateful for showed up in my life. As I felt more grateful in life, I began to feel happier. I felt hope. I felt joy. I felt optimism. And ultimately I felt the desire to serve others to the best of my abilities.

Who knows what you'll discover about yourself when you make #gratitude a part of your life!

Live In The Now

With the start of a new year I've been thinking about how important it is to live in the now.

But what does that mean anyway and how do you do it?

To me, living in the now means living fully engaged in every moment and enjoying the process as much as possible. It means understanding the past is over and the future, though important, only really matters when you love the process of creating it.

It's easy to get so caught up in what you're trying to accomplish that you forget to enjoy the process. Life isn't the future, nor is life the past. *Life is this moment.*

Now! And Now! And Now! This is life!

If you aren't enjoying the process of living then you aren't truly living.

Yes, all the moments strung together create your experience but it's how you interpret those moments that create the meaning you give life, that create your reality, and that determine whether you're enjoying the process of living or not.

That's a hard one for many to accept. After all, who likes to realize that their sadness, happiness, satisfaction, dissatisfaction, turmoil, or peace are solely the result of how they interpret their life, especially if their life isn't how they wish it was in one—or more—of those areas?

But it's true.

Part 1: Transformations

And once we accept that truth, we're in the position to consciously choose the meaning of our lives, we're in the position to live fully engaged and enjoy each moment.

But what about the events that hurt emotionally, physically, psychologically, or spiritually?

While those moments aren't enjoyable in the classical sense, they are a necessary part of your path. You can appreciate the lessons or seeds of growth that each of those moments contains. *It's up to you* to find the seeds of growth and plant them. Use them to help you become a better person. Use the knowledge and experience in those moments to help others. Give meaning that empowers you to those moments.

The meaning you give events in your life also impact your physical health.

In an interview with Anthony Robbins, Deepak Chopra discusses how two people can experience the same event and each give it different, even polar-opposite meanings. The meaning they choose to give the event determines how it impacts their physiology because nothing happens in the mind without also happening in the body. Depending on the meaning they give an event, they are either building up or tearing down their immune system. In short, your health is largely dependent on the meaning you give the events in your life.

Deepak Chopra goes on to say, "The meaning that you give to an event *is the event* because there is no such thing as actual reality. *There is only the perception of realty.*"

The meaning you give the events in your life become your physiology because each meaning produces chemical reactions. When you choose joy or gratitude or excitement as the meaning you give an event, your body produces a whole dif-

Another Slice of Pi

ferent set of chemicals than it does when you choose anger or ungratefulness or frustration.

But how do you learn to change the meaning of events?

The best thing I've discovered for changing the meaning of events in my life is to ask better questions about the events.

Instead of asking, "Why does this always happen to me?"

Try asking questions like; "What lesson is in this?" Or "How can I handle this better next time?" Or "How can I use this to help others?"

You can also ask, "What good can come of this?"

I encourage you to Live in the Now, Engage in Your Life, Accept Accountability for your Emotions, and Create Meanings that allow you to best Serve Others With Your Life!

Always Remember:
YOU ARE THE MASTER OF YOUR DESTINY!

Part 1: Transformations

Discover Your Passion

One of the most important things, that improves your ability to succeed in all areas of life, is discovering your passion and then doing it!

The simple truth is that discovering and living your passion brings you happiness and allows you to make a difference.

Discovering your passion has some great side effects too:

You can use your passion to help others!

You can use your passion to make money!

You can use your passion to have fun!

You can use your passion to live a fulfilled life!

But You Can't Figure Out How to Use Your Passion to Do These Things Until You Know What It Is.

Seriously, how do you know what your passion is? I mean, sure...there are things you enjoy doing, but are they things you're really passionate about?

Sometimes it is hard to know the difference between your true passion and something that's a temporary flash of excitement. Emotions can be misleading. What feels like passion today might not be your true passion.

Have heart though, because there are a few sure-fire ways to tell the difference between plain excitement and real passion.

First, you must figure out what your passions are.

Another Slice of Pi

If you want to discover your passion, then keep reading. But I warn you, this takes a little work. So if you really don't care what your passion is...then you might want to skip the rest of this post.

The first thing I'd like you to do is take a piece of blank paper and write "My Passions" on the top of it--if you need to use more than one piece that's okay too. Now think of the top ten things you most enjoy doing and write them down. Make sure you leave an inch or two free underneath each item. They don't need to be in any particular order either. The important thing is to get them on the page.

Go ahead and do it now.

*
*
*
*
*
*
*
*
*
*
*
*
*
*
*
*
*

Are you done?
Good.

Part 1: Transformations

Now take another piece of paper and write this:

"I would love to _____ !"

Fill in the blank with each passion you wrote down and read it out loud.

Do this for every passion on your list. Pay attention to your feelings when you read the statement. At least one of the passions you've listed will make your heart sing!

Which ones give you a jolt of happiness when you read them? Mark these with a star.

Now you have your list of passions and you've separated them into two groups. The group that you didn't put stars by are still things you'll want to do. They are things you enjoy. They aren't your real passions though. And that means you might have a harder time staying motivated about them.

The items with stars are your passions. Motivation is easier with these because you love doing them! But which one of them is The One, the Passion that carries your life to the next level and does the most good in the process?

Here's how you find out.

I'll use this sample list:

Exercise

Singing

Dancing

Quilting

Writing

Start with each one and compare it to the others in the list. Ask yourself, "If I had to choose between this Exercise and Singing, which would I choose?" Mark the answer and then ask the same question with Exercise and Dancing. Go through the list comparing Exercise to each one.

Do this with each passion on your list.

Another Slice of Pi

Which passion stood above the others as the thing you would always choose?

That's the passion to focus on. That's the passion that ignites you and breathes life into your dreams. That's the passion that sings greatness into your soul.

And the best part is this. Now that you know which passion moves you more than anything else, you can do it!

Part 1: Transformations

Three Critical Things about Changing Your Life

That You Might Not Know...

Change is Always Possible.

There are some who feel that change is out of reach to some, perhaps even forbidden. They promote the idea that some people just can't change or that once a person has done a certain thing, they're doomed to repeat that behavior for eternity...

This is a complete fallacy.

EVERYONE CAN CHANGE. EVERYONE HAS THAT POWER. It's part of being human.

And that brings us to the next point:

You Have to Truly Want to Change.

This is the place where most people get hung-up. They think they want to change their behavior—and their lives—but they're unwilling to do what's necessary to change their psychology. And truthfully, all change that lasts comes from a change in your personal psychology. That means a change in your thought processes, a change in your beliefs, and a change in your focus.

People who are unwilling to do what's necessary to create lasting change...either don't really want to change or they associate more pain with changing than they do with staying the same. They're often in love with the idea of changing and creating a better life but satisfy themselves with thoughts of change instead of taking action.

You can make changes in your life for a short time. But let's avoid fooling ourselves, unless you create change from within, the changes usually won't last.

You Must Take Action.

There is no way to stress this enough. For lasting change in your life *you must take action!* It isn't enough to read about it or to go to seminars or even to get therapy. You Must Take Action! You must apply the things you lean and discover. You must step into the uncomfortable, sometimes dark corners of your psyche and examine what you find. Then *you must choose a better path.*

I'll be completely transparent here. Changing your life can be painful. Sometimes it's easy to wonder if you'll ever make it. Sometimes it feels like you're being ripped apart from the inside when you realize how distorted your perception of reality was. Sometimes you might feel like giving up. When you feel overwhelmed, depressed, like you'll never succeed... Just remember that *You Can Do It!*

You Can Change!

And I Promise You This: No matter how difficult the path of personal transformation is for you; It Is Worth It! *You Are Worth It!* You'll look back in a few months (or years) and breathe a deep sigh of relief because you'll understand now that the path you walked was the necessary path for you to become the best version of yourself.

Part 1: Transformations

Are You Withholding Your Gifts?

Do you have a gift or talent that you might use to help others?

Are you using it?

If not, why not?

Are you afraid that you aren't good enough or that your idea isn't good enough?

I'd like to share a personal story that shows how I overcame the fear of using my gifts to help others.

As I wrote my first Self-Help Book, I had times when I thought, WHO DO YOU THINK YOU ARE TO WRITE A BOOK TO HELP OTHERS?

When that happened, I always redirected my thoughts to how much good my eBook will do and how much it will help others. But the thoughts kept coming back.

Then one day it hit me and the question, "Did God made a mistake giving me this knowledge and the ability to help others with it?" popped into my mind.

I didn't have to ponder that for long, "No. I believe God knew what he was doing." was my answer.

Next came this tough realization, "How selfish and small am I acting if I choose to withhold my gifts from the world?" And that was followed by, "Who am I to tell God he was wrong in giving me these gifts?"

For me, that was the end of any doubts about whether I was worthy to use my gifts to help others or whether I should pay any heed to fear. At that point I knew that even if I only touched one life, at least one person was better off for my efforts.

AND THAT'S ALL I NEED.

Look at, listen to, or feel what's in your heart. What does it tell you about the positive impact you can have on others?

Now, whether you believe in God or any higher power is beside the point. All you have to do is this; ask yourself the question, "Am I acting selfish and small by withholding my gifts from the world?"

ARE YOU?

Only you can answer that question. But if you think about it, I'm sure you'll realize at least one thing you can do to use your natural talents to help others.

Helping others can be as simple as posting an inspirational story or poem on your blog. It could be teaching someone how to do something. It might be singing for a friend or neighbor. It could be speaking to groups of people. It can be writing a book. It might be inventing something. It might even be giving a kind word to someone, acting in a movie that makes people laugh, or recording an album that lifts people's spirits. The list goes on and on.

The truth is that whatever your gift or talent, there is a way to use it to help others. All you have to do is ask your subconscious mind to help you find it.

Try this. If you feel stymied about how you can help others, then right before you go to bed kindly ask your subconscious, "Please help me discover how I can help others." Then go to sleep. The next morning or sometime the next day you will have inspiration about what you can do.

Now, this next bit is important. When you get that inspiration, ACT ON IT! This teaches you to trust your instinct and it tells your subconscious that you appreciate its efforts.

So, the next time you feel inspired to do something that will positively touch the lives of others, do it. And if you hear the small voice of fear or doubt whispering in your mind, just ask yourself the following questions:

- "Am I acting selfish and small by withholding my gifts from the world?"

- "Do I think (God, The Universe, My higher power) was wrong to give me these gifts and talents?"

- "Who am I to tell (God, The Universe, My higher power) that (He, She, or It) was wrong to give me these gifts and talents?"

If you do these things, you'll start to experience success in your life like you've never imagined.

Is it Hard to Be Happy?

I've been listening to an audio book. And while I appreciate and agree with most of what the author says, I did a triple-take when he said that it's very hard to be happy because there are a lot of things you must do to feel happy.

I disagree wholeheartedly with that stance.

One of the things I've learned on my path, which has been very rocky at times, is that happiness is a choice. And to me, it's an easy choice.

Yes, Happiness is Easy!

It's as simple as this: Find joy in the way your life is right now. That means think of the things that are how you want them to be. Think of the things you're grateful for. Think of the beauty of each moment as it happens. Live in the present instead of anchored to the past or searching for the future.

The only time you'll truly feel unhappy is when you're focusing on things that aren't how you want them to be.

- If you were abandoned by a parent and you spend a lot of time thinking about how unfair that is, then you'll feel unhappy.

Part 1: Transformations

- If you're single and you constantly think of how you wish someone was in your life, you'll feel unhappy.

- If you're out of work and you keep thinking about how horrible that is, then you'll feel unhappy.

- If you were injured or have a disability and think about all the things you could do if your body worked perfectly, then you'll feel unhappy.

Those are just a few examples of things you could choose to feel unhappy about. But the important thing to understand is that while feeling sad is natural at times, wallowing in sadness isn't. Wallowing in sadness is like complaining that a cactus is hurting you while squeezing it harder and harder...

So if you're feeling sad, thank the feeling for the message it's giving you because it's an action signal—a signal that you must take action! Then ask yourself what you can do to either change the situation or how you feel about the situation.

You MIGHT:

- Meditate and send thanks to the parent who abandoned you—for giving you life.

- Join clubs, organizations, or participate in activities where you might meet someone with similar interests and hobbies.

- Print up a resume, dress nicely, and hand deliver your resume to 5 to 10 different business a day. Then

Another Slice of Pi

check back in with the ones who seem interested about once a week. You'll land a job in no time. (I've done this in the past and it not only works, it gives a great first impression to employers.)

- Think of all the things you can do. If possible, find ways of exercising that increase your flexibility and mobility. Feel gratitude for the fact that you have a fully functioning mind.

- Make a gratitude list. This is one of my personal favorites! Just take a minute and write down at least 10 things you're grateful for. It does wonders to shift your mood.

- You can even go sit in nature and bask in its beauty for a while. Or sit under the stars and feel awestruck at the fact that your body is made of the same elements as those distant lights twinkling in the heavens.

No matter what your situation there is always something you can do to shift your focus from what you lack to what you have. That means there's always some action you can take to help you focus on happiness.

That's right, You Can Always Choose Happiness!

Part 1: Transformations

Healing Your Past

Many people carry painful past experiences with them like badges of honor. It's as if they say, *I survived this and that gives me meaning*. And that's okay. But what does it do to their life moving forward?

That depends on the meaning they give the event they survived.

The very idea of *surviving* something implies that it could have destroyed you. Some things can destroy us emotionally, some physically, some spiritually, and some cognitively. But unless an event ends your life or removes your ability to think cohesively, you always have control over the meaning you give it.

I know, I said that already. That's because it's important. So please pay attention and remember this:

You Always Have Control Over The Meaning You Give Events.

And that's *key to healing your past!*

Even now, if something terrible happened to you in the past, you can make the choice to give it a different meaning. You have the power to change something from an anchor that holds you captive in the past to a sail of hope that carries you into your brilliant future. And it can be as simple as asking

Another Slice of Pi

yourself the question, *What meaning can I give this (that event) that will empower me and help others?*

Let's do this together.

WARNING: YOU MIGHT WANT SOMEONE WITH YOU FOR MORAL SUPPORT—AND TO HELP YOU STAY IN THE PRESENT MOMENT—WHEN YOU DO THIS THE FIRST FEW TIMES. A COUNSELOR, THERAPIST, OR GOOD FRIEND ARE ALL GREAT CHOICES. IF NONE OF THOSE ARE AVAILABLE, YOU CAN START WITH A SMALLER EVENT, SOMETHING THAT'S NAGGING INSTEAD OF DEVASTATING. ONCE YOU MASTER THIS TECHNIQUE IT GETS EASIER TO DO AND IN TIME YOU'LL BE ABLE TO DO IT AT WILL AND YOU'LL EVEN DO IT WITH EVENTS AS THEY HAPPEN.

Think of something from your past that's painful to recall:

Here's mine. This is something I haven't thought of in years and when I remembered it I felt that emotional twinge that tells me I've never fully dealt with it.

When I was eight I had a step-father who thought it was a good idea to show my older brother and me just how powerful a 44-magnum handgun was. So he took us into the woods near our home and found a wild rabbit that was peacefully eating with its back to us.

He pulled out his 44, took aim, and shot the rabbit. The rabbit vanished in a puff of fur. To see that innocent life ended so violently was horrifying enough, but as I fought to hold back my tears—because I knew they were a sign of weakness to him—he walked my brother and me over to the place the rabbit had been just moments before. Then he laughingly showed us the pitiful remains of the small animal. I'll spare you the details.

Part 1: Transformations

At the time I felt scared, small, and powerless. Whether it was his intent or not, killing that rabbit in front of me and my brother felt like a deliberate display of power, like a threat from a man who easily outweighed me by two-hundred pounds, and who I feared already. I also felt sad at the senseless taking of the small animal's life.

Since I'm doing this with you, I'll now ask myself the question, ***"What meaning can I give this that will empower me and help others?"***

THE MEANINGS I CHOOSE NOW ARE THESE:

I learned valuable lessons that day, that help me and allow me to better serve others.

- I learned that in the core of my being I know how valuable life is and that it should never be wasted—no matter how small or seemingly insignificant it is.

- I learned about the power of empathy. I truly felt for that small creature and mourned for its passing.

- I learned how something that might seem trivial to one can have life-altering meaning for another. That means we should always be cognizant of the potential impact of our actions on others.

- I learned that we should never abuse our power. No matter who we are or what we can do, we should never deliberately harm others.

Another Slice of Pi

So, with these new meanings I forgive my step-father and now release the pain of the event.

I sincerely hope you try this method. It can be scary, it can even be painful. But if you do it carefully, in the presence of those who can help uplift and support you, I think you'll find it works wonders in healing your past, giving greater meaning to your present, and opening your sails to an amazing new future.

Part 1: Transformations

What is Living, Really Living?

Is the mere fact that you're alive, living? Or is it doing something with your life? Is truly living a quest, like the pursuit of knowledge, of power, of humility, of perfection, of living in service to others, of discovering spiritual truth?

Perhaps it's a combination of all these things. But I believe the real question is, "HOW DO YOU USE THE TIME YOU'RE GIVEN?" because it's one thing to think you know what living really means and it's another to put that in practice.

As you approach life, do you take each day by storm or sit idly by as the world spins beneath your feet?

There's a gap between existing and living, a place where many are trapped. Idleness beckons us with seemingly important things. It speaks to us with fun and distraction—often at other's expense. Some people even laugh at the pain and misfortune of others and call it fun... Things like video games, online communities, movies, internet videos, even watching sports or a television series, beg for our attention and can keep us from doing things that matter.

But who's to say what's wasted time? Who decides if the things we do matter? And why does it matter if they make a difference or not?

Ultimately The Answers to These Questions Come From Within.

For me, wasted time is time spent doing things that don't actively make a difference. That difference might be in my life, my family's lives, or the lives of people I've never met. The key is that as long as I'm moving forward and doing something that has a positive impact, I'm using my time well, I'm living well. Let's use meditation as an example. Some people might feel that meditating is wasted time because you're sitting still, doing nothing for ten to twenty minutes. For me, daily meditation is a gateway to peace and creativity. It opens my heart, mind, and soul to the greater truths of life. When I meditate regularly, my writing flows easily, ideas come freely, and I'm a much calmer, nicer person. In that regard my practice of daily meditation has a positive impact on those I interact with and those who read my books and blog.

So, even though I'm sitting there doing nothing—to all outward appearances—for me meditation is definitely time well used.

Now, that same time could be used to watch videos or shows or play games. The time invested is the same. But unless those things are somehow making life better for others or me, then what's the point?

What about play? Is that wasted time?

We need to play, to have unstructured free time where we can reset emotionally and physically from the normal routine. For me that's time on my skateboard ramp in my backyard or hiking in the mountains with my family, exercising, watching a good movie, or reading a great book. But the secret is this; play should enhance your life instead of overtaking it.

Part 1: Transformations

And the best way to live is when your work is play. That's how I feel when I'm writing, like I'm playing!

So one difference between living and simply existing is how you use your time. What's another difference?

Gratitude!

Do you appreciate the small moments in your life? Do you notice the beauty that surrounds you? Are you grateful for the things you have, even the little things like...breathing and the fact that your heart is still beating?

When you feel gratitude for everything in your life, you not only appreciate life more, you also live from a place of love and connection—with those around you and your world. When you live in a state of gratitude you simply get more of everything from life. And that's truly living!

Ultimately we're the judge of our actions. We know in our hearts if we're fulfilling our higher calling or simple wading through the mire. We know if we live in gratitude or if we keep a tally of everything that's wrong in our lives.

WHAT WILL YOU DO TODAY, RIGHT NOW; TO MAKE SURE YOU'RE REALLY LIVING?

Getting Traction After Change

Whether we're changing our internal beliefs, behaviors, or character traits, waiting for the results of our new patterns to manifest can feel like we're wandering through a dark forest. The results of our internal shift seem elusive, like beams of sunlight swallowed in fog. That's because there's usually a time lag between our internal changes and the external manifestation of these changes.

That's what I call "Getting Traction."

The time it takes to get traction with your new trait, belief, or behavior depends a lot on how drastic the change is from your old ways. Basically, it takes time for the new trait, behavior, or belief to filter into your reality. The bigger the change, the longer it can take. That doesn't mean that dramatic changes can't happen instantly. They can and they do. It just means that the manifestation of these changes can take some time to show up in your life.

This is a critical time for a lot of people. When they don't see immediate results, they might get discouraged and think, "I was wrong." Or "I must not be doing it right." Or "Maybe I haven't truly changed." Sometimes they even give up and, in time even go back to their old ways. And that IS tragic because they've already made the change! They're just a short time from realizing the amazing results of the change!

Part 1: Transformations

Think of it this way. Would you get discouraged if the seed you planted yesterday wasn't fully grown today? Not if you knew anything about seeds and how they grow. So why would you get frustrated when the seed of change you planted didn't produce results overnight?

The most important thing you can do when you've made a dramatic change in your beliefs, behaviors, or character traits is to have faith that the change will bear fruit. And I promise it will—as long as you remain steadfast in the change you've made or the belief you adopted.

If you find yourself doubting that the change you made was real, STOP! That's like cutting away at the roots of your new change-seed. If you persist in doubting, the seed of change can die. I know you want to keep the seed of change alive so it can grow into its full manifestation.

So when you find yourself doubting the power of your new belief, behavior, or character trait, just remind yourself that it's growing and KEEP BELIEVING IN YOURSELF. KEEP BELIEVING IN YOUR POWER TO CHANGE. And remember that all lasting changes are internal before they manifest on the outside.

Another Slice of Pi

The Real Problem with Labels

Have you ever been told that you're a looser, a quitter, fat, sloppy, skinny, ugly stupid, lazy, clumsy, no good, a liar, you'll never change, or that you're too this or too that? Seriously there are so many mean and hurtful things people say about others that it's astounding.

Sometimes we're told these things by people who are trying to hurt us. Mostly this is because they've learned that hurting others is a way to feel better about themselves, because they believe that if they tear others down enough, it lifts them up. Yeah, I know, that's a bizarre behavior.

The real kicker is that many of these labels are offered us by people we love, people that matter to us, who are acting out flawed behavioral scripts. Someone can care for you and still say mean things, they can throw labels at you when their angry, frustrated, or hurting that they'd never dream of using normally.

But why they do it is a topic for another post because why they do it has nothing to do with you. What really matters is what you do with these labels when they're offered to you.

That's right. No one can give you a label but you!

So the question is, "Are you going to accept all the labels you're given?"

I hope you said, "No!"

Part 1: Transformations

The truth is; some labels can be helpful and some are harmful. The real problem with labels is that if you start believing them, they can become your identity. Once a label becomes your identity your subconscious mind starts finding ways to make sure your behavior matches that belief. The belief in a personal label can be so powerful that a harmful label can easily destroy lives while an empowering label can create amazing successes.

So be very careful what labels you accept.

What to do if Someone Offers You a Label

When someone tells you you're _____ (you fill in the blank). You have the choice to accept their opinion as fact, to disregard it completely, or to reflect on whether there is any truth in their opinion.

If it's something blatantly mean and hurtful, then just throw it out. Realize that they're acting out a behavioral script they learned to cope with anger, hurt, or other stresses. This never makes the mean or hurtful behavior right or acceptable. It just helps you keep it in perspective.

You might say, "Thank you." Or, "I'm sorry you feel that way." You can stay calm and remind yourself that you're different than that label. You can ignore the comment entirely. You can also respectfully leave and resume the conversation when the other person calms down.

The key when refusing a label is to remain calm and let it slide on by. Even if you explore the possibility that there might be some truth to what they said, you can do it in a calm manner. When you get emotional about the label you give it focus. That gives it power because your subconscious mind uses emotion and focus to determine how important something is.

So stay calm and remember that *you are who you choose to be.*

What if the label is an empowering one, something that builds you up? Thank the person. Feel free to accept these labels when they align with your path, and if you do, then *get excited* that the person thinks *You're Smart, You're Strong, You're Healthy, You're Persistent, You're Clean, You're Powerful, You're Kind, You're Graceful, You're Honest*...Etc. Having a powerful emotional response to an empowering label helps it stick and that helps it become a belief.

Remember; *Your Beliefs Shape Your World.*

There is another layer to labels and we'll discuss that later. For now, remember to throw them out unless they serve you and keep the empowering ones you want.

Part 1: Transformations

Stepping Through Fear

If we want to grow we have to be willing to get uncomfortable. It's really that simple. No Discomfort = No Growth. Sometimes we're afraid of the discomfort though. We act like it can hurt us. When fear becomes part of the growth equation things can get complicated fast.

Why?

Fear can sidestep our ability to think clearly. Uncontrolled, it can turn us into blithering idiots, or worse shut down our humanity and turn us into vicious animals. Fear can also paralyze, freeze us into patterns of behavior that prevent growth and that prevent action. When we fear change, our ability to grow quickly diminishes because we start avoiding things that make us uncomfortable, things we fear, the very things that can help us change.

Understand that fear can be useful. The fear that comes from something like stepping into oncoming traffic is very real and should be heeded, while the fear of public speaking is illusionary and can be discarded—meaning that no matter how scary public speaking might seem, it won't physically hurt you.

In both cases fear is an action signal. It tells you that to get back to safety. But as you realize, when it's illusionary fear, safety really means your comfort zone.

How Can You Beat Fear?

The best way to beat fear is to learn to step through it. Stepping through fear means you experience the fear and do it anyway. It means training yourself to think clearly in the midst of fear instead of letting fear paralyze you. You can step through your fear with small things at first, and always with things that are done as safely as possible.

For example: If you fear public speaking, you could ask a small group of friends to let you tell them a story. Just have them sit on one wide of the room while you stand on the other. Then tell a short funny story from your childhood or from work. When you're comfortable with that, you'll move to larger groups. In no time you'll forget why you were ever afraid because you'll enjoy the experience of connecting with others in the way that only public speaking provides.

Here's an example from my life.

Over The Edge

A few months ago I had the opportunity to go rappelling for the first time in over a decade. As we approached the top of the cliff I started to feel a little nervous. It had been awhile since I'd been that close to a drop off of more than 10 or 15 feet, this one was a little over 130 ft. To put that in perspective, that's like standing on the roof of a 10 story building.

My heart started to pound. My palms got sweaty. I felt fear rising. DO I REALLY WANT TO DO THIS? I wondered and considered walking away. But then I reminded myself, "This is no big deal. I used to clean windows on high-rises. I can do it!"

Part 1: Transformations

I'd like to say I went first. I didn't. I was the second one up. As my friend, who'd organized the trip, showed me exactly how to connect the rappel device to the rope and then to my harness, the fear monkeys went crazy in my head. It was like standing in the middle of a hundred monkeys, all barking, screaming, and threatening me, telling me all the horrible possibilities, demanding I give up.

SHUT UP! I mentally shouted as I edged backward, toward the gap. There I stood, 130 feet yawning beneath me. My feet planted on the edge of the cliff face, but not committed yet. I could still call it off.

Despite the cacophony of my fear monkeys, I took another step, then another. And then I'd passed the point of no return. The only way off that cliff was straight down.

The fear monkeys didn't quiet much on my first decent. Though I enjoyed it, I was also desperate to reach the ground. When I got to the bottom I felt waves of relief wash over me.

I did it!

Then I thought, *Okay, that's done we can go home now.* And I knew the fear monkeys were still trying to control the situation. I wasn't about to let that happen. So I went back to the top of the cliff and rappelled again. In fact, I took three turns that day.

Did my fear monkeys ever go away? No. They quieted until they were mostly background noise. But they still raged a few times.

The important thing is that I faced my fear and did it anyway. I remained calm and rational despite fear and controlled it instead of letting it control me.

Another Slice of Pi

You can too. It might not be a literal cliff that challenges you, but fear can make it feel that way. If you start small and do the thing you fear, it will get easier with each doing. In time it might even go away!

Part 1: Transformations

How to Feel Happy

Do You Ever Struggle With Happiness?

There's a Simple Method That Helps You Feel Happier!

And it's not later. You'll FEEL HAPPIER RIGHT NOW! When you make this a habit, it truly shifts your life.

So, what is it? How will you feel happy regularly, regardless of life's twists and turns?

Learn to change your focus!

What? C'mon there has to be more to it than that.

Seriously, It's Really that Easy.

Every situation has both positive and negative aspects. Even situations that are really crappy have positive things about them. It might be something as simple as a lesson to help you avoid that type of situation in the future. It could be gaining insight that allows you to help or better empathize with others. It could even be an opportunity to finally change one's life.

Most situations aren't dramatic in the difference between their positive or negative aspects. Most things are simply an easy choice where to look.

For example; Stephen Covey told a story about a time that he was riding on a subway. Another passenger, a man, had four unruly children with him. The children were upsetting other passengers with their noise and chaotic activity and

Another Slice of Pi

their father was ignoring them. Finally Dr. Covey had enough and asked the man to please control his children.

The man looked at him and said that he was sorry. The children's mother had just passed away and they were on the way home from the hospital. The kids just didn't know how to deal with it and were acting out.

Dr. Covey, with new insight in the situation, immediately changed his focus and started helping with the children. He also related in the story that he learned a great deal about the importance of empathy that day.

So What are The Positives in The Situation?

Dr. Covey learned a lesson about empathy and was able to help another person during his time of trial.

For the man and his children, I imagine it was receiving the help and compassion of a stranger during a time of great need.

It's like the comparison between the rose and the thorns. Both are there. Where are you looking?

We've Been Trained

I know, we've been trained—at least in Western Society—to look for happiness in things and events. Often we get caught up in the misconception that we can feel happy when... (You fill in the blank)

And that's one of the biggest lies of all. We can feel happy right now. You can feel happy this instant. All you have to do is choose to allow yourself to experience the positive in whatever situation you're in right now. Even if the positive is realizing that you'd better change your situation!

Part 1: Transformations

Do What's Right—Because it's Right!

First off, let's define Good or Right behavior as behavior that's healthy emotionally, psychologically, physically, & spiritually. A good measure is the Golden Rule—Do unto others as you would have them do unto you.

Now, think about the good people you know; the one's you know are good because their consistent actions prove it. Do you think they're good because they're afraid of getting in trouble? Do you think they're good because they're afraid of breaking the rules?

Of course not!

They act the way they do because they have an internal compass with True North pointing straight to Goodness. It's part of who they are. Perhaps they developed this intrinsic understanding and desire to do good as children. Maybe they learned this as adults.

But the key is this:

They Do What's Right, Because It's Right, Because it Comes From Within.

WHY IS THIS IMPORTANT?

When people do what's right because they fear repercussions, they're either masking behavior, they don't understood why certain behaviors are harmful, or they haven't learned to cope differently with certain situations and are just doing their best to conform.

Take the person who texts and drives for example. They might avoid the behavior as best they can because they don't want to get in trouble. But if they truly understood that texting while driving can either take another's life or their own life, they simply wouldn't do it. They might know it in their head, they might even have the statistics memorized, but until they truly understand the danger and internalize the value of human life they'll most likely revert to the behavior occasionally.

Over a long period of time following rules or doing what's right because of fear can create habits of healthy behavior. But it's not a method that always develops an internal compass pointed toward emotionally, spiritually, and psychologically healthy behavior. That only happens when the individual internalizes changes and truly understands why they are necessary. And that happens with soul-searching and a true desire to change.

How Do We Affect Internal Change, and Realign Our Internal Compass?

Here's one simple method to start:

First: IDENTIFY THE BEHAVIOR THAT NEEDS TO CHANGE.

Reflecting on what's causing consistent conflict in your life is a good place to start. If you're unsure then ask a friend or loved one. And be ready for their answer because chances are you won't like it. But if you're committed to changing your life, you'll listen.

Part 1: Transformations

(Admittedly, this part can be difficult at first. We all have blind spots and it can help to have a trusted therapist, counselor, or coach on this part of your journey. The farther you get on the road to wholeness the easier this part gets because you gain self-awareness.)

Second: ASK YOURSELF THE FOLLOWING QUESTIONS:

- If your behavior is directed toward others, ask:

    - How would I feel if someone else treated me that way?

- If your behavior is directed at yourself—self-inflicted—ask:

    - Would I treat others that way?

- If you would never treat others that way, then ask:

    - Why would I treat myself like that?

    - How would I feel if someone else treated me that way?

    - Would I tolerate it? (We often treat ourselves much harsher than we'd ever accept from others)

Now that you've gained some awareness about why the behavior is unhealthy or outright harmful, it's time for the biggest step in this process.

Another Slice of Pi

Ask yourself:

- What will I do differently in the future if I find myself in that—or a similar—situation?

Take a few minutes and write down what you'll do differently in the future. Think about how you'll respond. How you'll treat others. How you'll come to a peaceful resolution. How you might avoid the situation entirely.

It also helps to envision the scenario and see, hear, and feel yourself resolving it in an emotionally healthy manner.

Part 1: Transformations

Walk Your Own Path

How often do others tell you that you should do this with your life or you should do that with your life? I know it's happened to me a lot over the years. And I imagine it's happened to you.

Generally the people giving the advice are well meaning. And their motives vary. Sometimes they tell you that, "That's where the money is!" Sometimes they tell you that, "It's the path to happiness!" or, "It's the way to be successful!" or, "It's the path to true spirituality and inner peace!" And that's great. The path that's working for them is wonderful for them. But...

It Doesn't Matter Where They Think The Path Leads If It's Not Your Path.

You may want success. You may want happiness. You may want wealth. You may want greater spirituality and inner peace. You may want a combination of all these, or you may want something completely different. But whatever you want, even if it's exactly what someone else is telling you their path leads to, your path still might be different because you are different, unique, with your own skills and talents and dreams and desires.

You Are You. Your Path is Your Path. No One Else Can Walk It. No One Else Can Tell You What It Is.

Sure, others may guide you. But you have to discover your own path. Once you're on your true path you'll find guides, mentors, and way posts to keep you heading the right direction. And you must ignore those telling you your path isn't right. Besides, how could they possibly know whether your path is right? It's your path, not theirs.

What if You Haven't Discovered Your True Path?

Take a few minutes and reflect on the things that bring you the most joy in life. I'm talking true joy. What really makes your heart sing? What moments are filled with pure bliss, where time seems to stand still and the world falls away leaving you in a perfect moment?

These are your passions and they're clues to your true path. Some might call it your calling in life instead of your path. That's okay. Whatever you call it, it's yours and you should live it.

How Do I Live My True Path?

The best way I've found to start living your true path, to really walk it, is to ask yourself the following question, "How can I use my passions to help others or to make the world a better place?"

Now Go Do It! Get out there and Walk Your Own Path!

Part 1: Transformations

Afraid to Take The Shot

I was listening to a sports talk show Sunday morning—while I drove to an event I was writing an article about—and the host was talking about Kentucky Basketball and their so-far undefeated 2015 season. Specifically he was celebrating the fact that they seem very relaxed under pressure.

They Aren't Afraid to Miss.

THAT'S THE SECRET OF THEIR SUCCESS, he went on, BECAUSE IT ALLOWS THEM TO FOCUS ON THE SHOT AS IT UNFOLDS INSTEAD OF THE CONSEQUENCES OF THE SHOT. Those might not be his exact words, but that's the idea. I was so impressed by this that I immediately pulled over and wrote it down.

That got me thinking about how many times we miss in life because we're afraid of missing.

When we focus on the consequences of a shot we're taking, we add fear and ego to the equation. We add pressure. The sHOT we're taking may be something we've done successfully hundreds or thousands of times before, but when we start thinking about what happens if we "miss" or even if we "make it" we remove ourselves from the Flow and rhythm that helps us succeed. As you understand, this increases the odds of missing because it can throw our whole system (or process) out of whack. Worse, it can cause us to start second guessing ourselves.

Second Guessing Ourselves Can Quickly Lead to Disaster.

I had a poignant example of this in my life when I was younger. I was called upon by two of my friends to be their third fighter in a team martial arts competition. They knew me. They knew I was a great fighter. They knew my work ethic and had seen my dedication to the art for years. It was an honor that they chose me to act as clean up in the sparring competition.

But I'd never been in a sparring match before and I was nervous...

Going into my match we had a 10 point lead. All I had to do was maintain the point spread they'd gotten in their matches. That was it. Easy...right?

I'll spare you the details—even though I remember them clearly even now. We had a 10 point lead going into the match...and a 5 point deficit coming out of it.

I was slaughtered. We lost because I didn't maintain the lead. And worse, I'd let down my friends.

What happened?

I'd put so much pressure on myself to do well that I locked up physically. I second guessed everything. I didn't trust my body to react the way I'd trained it to over the years. I was tight, jerky and mechanical in my movements, and completely out of Flow.

Essentially I was so afraid of missing, of failing, that I couldn't function.

It was so bad that my Martial Arts instructor came up to me after the match and said, "Who was that? That wasn't Roland. You could have easily beaten him."

How Do We Overcome Our Fear of Missing The Shot?

Fear of missing is fear of failure. Like all fears, fear of failure can be conquered. Here are a few methods that'll get you past fear and back into the game.

- Build Confidence in your abilities by placing yourself in the situation—through repetition.

- Treat Each Event as an isolated instance.

- Do things you love.

Let's expand on these.

Build Confidence Through Repetition

The first time you do something your confidence might be low. Do it anyway! And then do it again and again.

When you do it, when you take the shot, focus on what went right and use that next time to make yourself better. Recognize the things that didn't work and adjust your technique in the future. There are few things that build confidence like repetition.

The thing is to realize that we're all imperfect. We make mistakes. And that's okay! We also have the power to actively learn and grow. So be gentle on yourself while you're learning. Give yourself permission to make mistakes and you'll learn faster. It's really simple; the more you do it, the better you'll get.

Treat Each Event (or Shot) as an Isolated Instance

This might seem to contradict the first point. But follow me on this: treating each shot—whether it's a sales pitch, a report you're writing, a painting or sculpture you're creating, or an actual shot in a game—as an isolated instance means simply to *let the past and future fall away and focus wholly on the task at hand. Appreciate* the moment as *now* and do what you know how to do.

Sure you bring all your knowledge and training with you. And then you release concern about the history behind the event—your shot—and release concern about the consequences or outcome. Just relax and let all the training or practice you've had guide you.

You can handle the results after the shot because you'll see them then. That's when you learn and grow. That's when you celebrate, or not. But during the shot, just let it unfold. Focus wholly on the shot and you'll be in Flow.

Do Things You Love

This is important because doing things you love increases your likelihood of doing them. Makes sense right? This is key because doing them—taking your shots—builds confidence and releases fear.

Part 1: Transformations

Luciano Pavarotti said, "People think I'm disciplined. It is not discipline. It is devotion. There is a great difference."

When you love what you're doing, when you're passionate about it, you're going to do it because you can't get enough of it. You live it and love it and breathe it! That means you continually take your shots! And remember, repetition is key to building confidence and releasing fear!

Now I know the next question is, "What about building confidence and releasing fear when I've never done something before?"

I'll cover that in my next blog post. So check back soon!

How to Build Confidence and Release Fear

How do you build confidence and release fear when you're doing something for the first time?

We've all been there. We have a new opportunity or find ourselves in a new situation, facing something we've never done before. We feel nervous or even scared that we'll mess it up. We lack confidence. But we want to do it. Or maybe we don't really want to do it; maybe it's something we feel we have to do.

Either way, we're there and it's a new experience. It can be nerve-wracking. But it doesn't have to be. *Whether doing something new is a good experience or not is completely up to you.*

Yeah, that's right. I know you might not want to realize that because it places you in the accountability seat for your life. But it's true. The meaning you give doing something new is your choice. You can *choose to interpret it as a wonderful opportunity to learn and grow.* Or you can think of it as a terrible, scary experience. Chances are you'll be somewhere in between. But *it's always your choice.*

Oh sure, you might still feel a little nervous—that's natural. But why not *enjoy the process of learning?*

So how do you do it? How do you approach a new experience with confidence while releasing fear?

Part 1: Transformations

Give Yourself Permission to Fail, to Mess Up, to Be Imperfect

What?

I thought we were talking about how to develop confidence and release fear in new situations?

We are. No one does something perfectly the first time they try. The fear associated with new things is usually caused by:

1. Fear of failing

2. Fear of embarrassment

3. Fear of ridicule

4. Fear of not being good enough

All of these fears can be alleviated with the understanding that failure is a natural part of the learning and growth process. Let's be clear, we're talking about failure as being imperfect, about trying our best while understanding that we might not get it right. We're talking about our commitment to learn and grow—so we'll do it better next time. So we pay attention, listen, and feel the things that work, while noticing the things that didn't, so we can improve with each effort.

Simply put, when you do something new while giving yourself permission to be imperfect, it releases fear. Heck, if you really mess it up, you might even laugh at yourself. And that's okay!

Another Slice of Pi

Giving yourself permission to be imperfect also helps with confidence because you can feel confident in your ability to learn and grow. Just think of all the things you've learned to do in your life. Really think about them. There are hundreds—probably thousands—of things you've learned how to do. So whether you've realized it before or not, YOU'RE REALLY GOOD AT LEARNING THINGS!

Why would this new thing be any different? You'll learn it. You'll grow with it. You'll be great at it in time... But only if you take that first step.

So *give yourself permission to fail* and *find confidence in your ability to learn and grow*!

Now get out there and try something new!

Part 1: Transformations

Never Argue for Your Weakness

Has someone ever told you about a weakness they have, something they can't do, or problems they're having, and then they go on to explain all the reasons they either can't change these things or have no control over them?

Have you ever done this yourself?

It's something I call arguing for your weakness. It's an unhealthy habit and quickly sabotages your success.

Why?

When a person starts telling others why they can't do something, change something, or why they have no control over a situation, they're coming from a place of victimhood. They're focusing on and reinforcing the negative aspects of situations and life. They're also forgetting that no matter what, they always have control of the meaning they give an event. And worse, they're nearly guaranteeing that things will never change for them—at least in that area of their life.

Understand that we all have something about ourselves that we'd like to change or something about our lives that we'd like to change. It might be something big, something that would dramatically improve our lives—if we just made the shift. It might be a little thing that no one but us would really notice. But it's there. And we know it.

We can approach these a few ways. When we look at these things, we can choose to see the parts that upset us. Or we can listen to the lessons, the things we can learn from the situation. We can also understand the inherent good and seek understanding of that.

What Can You Do?

The next time you discover yourself telling someone—or yourself—all the reasons you can't do something, why something you dislike is "Just the way it is", or why you have no control over any situation... STOP IT!

You Always Have Control Over the Meaning You Give Events.

You Always Have a Choice How You Respond.

It's Your Life.

You Choose Your Path.

Get out there and *Master Your Destiny!*

Part 1: Transformations

You'll Never Cure Hate with Hate

Hate is such an ugly thing.

Why is there so much of it in our world? What does it accomplish? Does it make the person who hates feel better? Does it solve any problems? Does it impart social, spiritual, economic, or personal change and growth?

What do you think?

Hate is bred from many things. It can come from intolerance, sadness, and anger. It can be learned—whole generations on our planet have hated others only because they were taught to. Hate can come from lack of empathy—those who fail to understand others sometimes fear them, which can lead to hate if they fail to seek understanding. Hate often comes from fear; fear of change, fear of harm, fear of the unknown, fear of pain...

No matter where hate's roots form, the plant they grow is withered and twisted, a blight on life's light. Hate sucks joy from life as quickly as the burning sun sucks water from the desert. And none can hate without damaging themselves more than the object of their hatred because to hate someone one must repeatedly think of the things they hate about them. To hate another, one must focus on them with burning anger and stoke those flames daily.

A Warning to Those Who Hate...It Consumes You, Devouring Love and Joy, Leaving an Empty Shell in the End.

IS THAT WHAT YOU WANT?

Of course not!

Hating another also gives them power over you because you'll find yourself shaping your life and actions based on decisions born of hatred... And answering hatred with hatred is no answer at all. That destroys both parties.

Imagine this, hate is like a stone. When you answer hate with hate it's like slamming two stones against each other. What happens? They chip or shatter.

LOVE IS LIKE WATER. When you throw the stone of hate into the water of love it sinks. Sure it splashes and breaks the surface, but then it sinks and the surface heals. In the end the water of love is undamaged and it embraces the stone of hate. It surrounds the stone of hate and wears it away. Given enough time the stone is gone and the waters of love flow on.

Think of this: Gandhi changed the world with love. Mother Theresa changed the world with love. Martin Luther King changed the world with love. And so have many others, perhaps not on such a grand scale, but they changed it nonetheless.

Sure, they may have hated how something was, but they didn't focus on the hatred. They used their feelings of disquiet and angst to fuel their desire to have a positive impact on the world. *They focused on changing the world through love.*

The only antidote for hate is love.

What are you going to do?

Part 2: Health & Fitness

Part 2: Health & Fitness

Get In Shape!

Since Fitness is a big part of my philosophy, I decided that every Saturday I'll post something Fitness related.

Here is the first installment. Enjoy!

You Want To Get in Shape...But Don't Know Where to Start.

Many people think you have to join a gym or buy expensive equipment. Well that's wrong!

You just have to start. Build a habit.

How?

Here's a sample workout you can follow for a few weeks to a month. It's a good jumping off point and requires no equipment.

After a while, you might want to start mixing up exercises or adding a different ones from the exercise list page. Just remember that Hindu pushups and Hindu squats are staple exercises—their benefits are more than just muscular.

Note: This is a starting workout regimen, unless you're in good shape, you should reach failure quickly

Day 1 Monday:
1 set Hindu pushups to failure
1 set Bicycle crunches to failure
1 set wrestlers bridge (10 to 30 sec)
1 set Hindu squats (half of failure reps)

Day 2 Tuesday:
1 set Hindu pushups (half of failure reps)
1 set Bicycle crunches (half of failure reps)
1 set Hindu squats to failure
1 set Wrestlers Bridge (30 sec to 1 minute)

Day 3 Wednesday:
1 set Hindu squats (half of failure reps)
1 set Wrestlers Bridge (10 to 30 sec)
1 set Crunches (your choice) to failure
1 set pushups (your choice) to failure

Day 4 Thursday:
   1 set crunches (same type as day 3) (half of failure reps)
   1 set pushups (same type as day 3) (half of failure reps)
1 set Wrestlers Bridge (30 sec to 1 minute)
1 set Hindu squats to failure

Day 5 Friday:
Repeat day 1

Day 6 Saturday:
Repeat day 2

Day 7:
Rest

Repeat the cycle for the next few weeks.
Start now!

Part 2: Health & Fitness

The Magic Pill

Is there a magic fitness pill?

Um...No.

Sorry, no gadget will do everything you need or hit every muscle group. No supplement, taken by itself without exercise, gives you Herculean strength or makes you agile and lightning fast. Results like that require consistent effort.

What about a magic weight reduction pill?

There are medications to help control diet and induce weight reduction. But the truth is these pills have side effects—just read the small print—and many of them create more issues than they solve. So I say no, there aren't any shortcuts to reaching your ideal weight.

It's simple. Do you eat more than you burn? If so, you'll gain weight. It might be slow, it might be fast, but it will happen. But the good news is this; if you eat slightly less than you burn, you'll reduce your waistline. If you add exercise to the mix, you'll build muscle and soon fit into those old jeans!

Here's my simple formula: If you want a fit, lean, and healthy body, then eat less and do some work. Or eat the same and do more work!

I know. It's not rocket science!

There are ways to add more activity in your day. Things like taking stairs instead of elevators, parking in the back of the store parking lot, even making sure you just move around your home, are great ways to add physical activity to your day.

These are great ways to increase the calories you burn without adding extra time to your daily routine.

But the most important thing you can do is figure out what you want. Find your reason for exercising, make goals, and give your workouts purpose! After all, it's easier to motivate yourself when you know what each workout means to you.

Some people workout to get stronger. Some people workout to get or stay lean. Some people workout to train for a sport. Some people workout out because they enjoy being healthy. But no matter your reason for working out; exercise benefits your health and improves your quality of life.

Start Now! No Excuses!

Part 2: Health & Fitness

Can Older People Get Fit?

I saw a "Special" on the Sunday morning news awhile back on older people getting in shape.

That's great, I thought. I think all people should be encouraged to exercise.

But then they had a specialist "Geriatric Doctor" on. She said that while a few "exceptions" may be able to maintain high levels of fitness when they're older, the majority of people shouldn't hope for those results.

What?

I have issues with this kind of thinking...

As soon as you say "I can't", you're right... At that point you're done.

Why is it the exception? Perhaps our older generation wasn't taught to stay healthy when they were younger. This might place them at a lower starting point but it hardly means they can't get in great shape.

Any one of any age can improve their fitness levels. If you shoot for the stars and hit the sun you'll still be in great shape. But if you listen to doctors—like the one who was on—and only shoot for the roof top, you might hit it. But it's a long way from the sun...

What's wrong with being the exception when health is the issue?

Nothing!

Another Slice of Pi

The best way to be in great shape when you are older, is to get in great shape now and either maintain it or always strive to improve it!

But if you're older now, you can still start. You can still improve your fitness and your quality of life. Sure, be smart about it. If you've never exercised, consult your physician and start slowly and cautiously. Then build over time.

But there's a difference between being smart about fitness and having low expectations.

What are you going to do?

Part 2: Health & Fitness

No Time for Cardio?

Many people think of Cardio and Strength training as two separate activities. But what if you have a busy life? What happens when you just have time to do one or the other?

Is there a way to get the best of both worlds?

Yup!

And it's simple too. But like most simple and effective things it takes *discipline and desire.*

Take your normal workout and decrease the resting time between sets to 1 minute. Or better yet, 30 seconds! (If you use a stopwatch it's easy to time yourself between sets.)

Now 30 sec to 1 minute might sound like a good rest between sets, but it'll kick your heart into high gear! And it has other benefits too. It reduces the total time of your workout, it gives you a deeper burn in the muscles being trained, and it gets your heart up to speed—and keeps it there for the whole workout. It also builds great discipline.

So if you want to have all the benefits of strength training and cardio, without taking the time to do both, make sure you reduce the time between your sets.

Go ahead, give it a try.

Commitment

A drop of water isn't much by itself. It's a small wet spot that vanishes before it's noticed. Maybe it's a frustration to the thirsty person licking at the mouth of their canteen.

But many drops of water combined can flood a house, wash away a hillside, even fill an ocean...

Commitment is the combination of individual events that fulfill a promise. I've promised myself I'd stay in great shape and be healthy and fit. I've made promises to others for different reasons. But all these things, whether to me or to others, are commitments that I made. Each commitment lives or dies by the actions I take every day. When I notice a commitment starting to wither, I give it extra effort until it's healthy and thriving again.

I challenge you to meet your commitments in all aspects of your life.

I challenge you to make the commitment to get in shape or stay in shape and to take the daily steps needed to give that commitment meaning. But most of all, I challenge you to persist and overcome when you struggle with commitment.

A commitment only dies when you stop trying.

Part 2: Health & Fitness

Start!

There was a time in my life when I could only do one pull-up. And no, I'm not talking about when I was a baby--though it's true that I couldn't do a pull-up then. I'm talking about six and a half years ago when I decided to get in shape and to finally shed my fat.

At that point all I could do was hang from the bar, struggle my way to the top and then hope for another pull-up. But I did just that!

OK, I didn't hope.

I believed! I believed and kept pulling. Every day I took one small step. By the end of a week I was doing two pull-ups. By the end of a month I was doing five. Now I do twenty to twenty five in a set.

The same principle works in all aspects of life. When you want to improve something, believe in yourself and just *start taking small steps*. Before you know it, your there!

I challenge you to start. Whatever your fitness goal, you'll never reach it unless you start. So get up right now and place your feet on the road to fitness. Then take a step, and another. Before you know it, you'll be amazed at your results.

Lower Back Pain...

Do you suffer with lower back pain?

You'd be surprised how many people answer "Yes".

I was one of those people. In the past I herniated two disks in my lower back. At first I was so concerned about Doing Something that would aggravate my injury, that I drastically limited my movement. I tried to hold my lower back ramrod straight all the time.

Then my lower back tightened up, which ironically increased the pain. I was "Injured". I limited my motion. My pain increased...

That went on for almost a year before I learned that strengthening my core alleviated most of the pain. Since then I've made sure my core muscles are strong and flexible. And it's amazing the difference that's made.

For nearly ten years I've been pain free!

But when I was overly concerned with re-injuring my lower back, I focused on the "injury" and my symptoms worsened. Thinking about it all the time meant I gave it attention. As I gave it more attention it hurt more. Then I thought about it more...

It became a self-fulfilling prophecy.

But once I learned there was an alternative—keeping my core strong and flexible. I thought about the "Injury" less. I thought about being strong and healthy more. That's when my back stopped hurting.

Part 2: Health & Fitness

But what I thought about wasn't the only ingredient in my recipe for a healthy, pain-free, back.

As I mentioned above, I strengthened my core muscles, started moving again, and stretched. Understand that motion is good for your body. When you stop moving your muscles tighten and atrophy. That makes them prone to injury. When you move and stretch regularly, your muscles gain strength and flexibility. That makes them resistant to injury.

It's also important that when you exercise do it because you want a healthy back and spine. Then your attention is in the right place.

Be smart about it too. If you have an injury, consult a physician, physical therapist, or alternative medicine practitioner about the exercises and stretches you can do. And then do them!

Personally I enjoy Bicycle Crunches, Wrestlers Bridge, Front Bridge, Hanging Knee-Ups, and many Yoga Poses. (Check out the Exercise List Page) Most of these are advanced exercises though. So the important thing is that you start where you can safely start.

Just remember:

Strong, Flexible Core = Pain Free Back!

http://www.rolandbyrd.co/bodyweight-exercise-list/

No Place for Pull-Ups?

My workout philosophy is mostly based on _Bodyweight Exercises_. And almost all bodyweight exercises can be done with no apparatus.

But what about *pull-ups*? If you don't want to buy a pull-up station where can you do them?

It's time to think like Jackie Chan. He doesn't let the fact that there aren't any knives, staves, or swords nearby stop him.

Nope! He'll take anything in sight and turn it into a devastating weapon.

So take a look around and see what you can turn into a *Fat Fighting Weapon*. Be creative!

Some of the places I've done pull-ups over the years are:

On a jungle gym

Hanging off of the second story walkway of a Motel

On the underside of open back stairs

Hanging from garage rafters

Hanging from a soccer goalpost

On a thick tree branch

On the top bar of a park swing set

There are more places and items that I've used, but I think you get the idea. If you have the desire, you'll find a way.

Part 2: Health & Fitness

The Power of Persistence!

Growth of any kind only comes with persistence. If you want to reduce your weight, start exercising and eat healthy foods. Then *keep it up! Make it a habit.*

Persistence *is* the magic ingredient. Persistence adds POWER!

The same goes for strength training or any type of fitness training. First *you must start,* then you must CONTINUE. Imagine the results you'll get if you only train in an on-again, off-again manner?

Are those the results you want?

Now imagine your ideal body after you've made a habit of consistent, focused training.

Those *are* the results you want!

So whether you train for a specific activity, to get stronger, or just to be in great shape, *remember to add that magic ingredient!*

Remember to be Persistent!

Want help developing Persistence? Read "Your Blueprint, Life by Design" and "Break Your Mold: The Art of Overcoming Patterns and Behaviors That Hold You Back".

http://www.rolandbyrd.co/books-by-roland-byrd/

What Do You Believe?

What do you believe about yourself?

Do you **believe** *you can get in shape?*

Do you **believe** *you can shed unwanted pounds?*

Do you **believe** *you can build lean muscle*?

Do you **believe** *you will stay lean and fit* once you reach your goal?

Do you **believe** *you will achieve any goal you set*?

If the answer to any of these is no, then you will struggle and most likely fall short of your goals. If *the answer is yes*, **YOU WILL SUCCEED!**

Like it or not, your subconscious mind works day and night to shape you into the person you believe you are. Because of this, self-belief is one of the most powerful tools you can use when changing your life. If you don't use it, *now is the time to start.*

Just follow these steps:

Think of how wonderful you feel now that you've reached your goal.

Think of all the things reaching your goal does for you.

Does it allow you to participate in activities that were out of reach before?

Do *you feel more confident*?

Do *you have more energy*?

Feel your *pure gratitude* now that *you've reached your goal.*

Part 2: Health & Fitness

Now that you're filled with feelings of gratitude, confidence, and joy—because you've reached your goal—form a picture or movie in your mind of who you are once you've reached that goal.

What do you look like?

How do you act?

How do you carry yourself?

Now attach your wonderful feelings of success to the picture or movie by feeling them while you focus on it.

Believe **YOU ARE THAT PERSON**.

REVISIT *the picture or movie* every morning and again before you go to sleep at night.

Do You Have a Routine?

A daily routine is a great way to maintain good habits. And when you want fitness as a way of life, you must create an exercise habit.

But what happens when your routine gets thrown out of whack?

If you aren't careful, a messed up routine can weaken a strong habit of exercise. How do you keep your exercise habit strong when your routine gets derailed?

The best answer is, *"Just do something!"* Do the exercises you can in the time you have available. Or make time and use available resources. The most important part of this is to realize that even a reduced workout is a workout, it's still a step down the path of fitness, and it will help keep your habits strong!

So stop making excuses and stay on track. You'll thank yourself later.

Part 2: Health & Fitness

Breathing and Exercise

For some reason most people hold their breath when they're moving weight—this includes weight lifting, bodyweight exercises, etc. They'll stop breathing while pushing or pulling because it feels like it helps move the weight. But in reality it cuts off the Oxygen supply and strains the diaphragm.

The best way to breathe while exercising—moving weight or bodyweight—is to breathe into your diaphragm during the relaxed or negative phase of the exercise and then breathe out steadily while contracting the muscles or doing the rep.

Take push-ups and pull-ups for example:

Push-ups: Breathe in as you lower your body toward the ground and then exhale steadily while pushing your body back to the start position.

Pull-ups: Breathe in while lowering your body—or at the bottom before the first rep—and then breathe out steadily while pulling yourself to the top of the movement.

It also helps to lightly contract the muscles of your core while breathing out. This gives extra support to your lower spine and helps tone your core.

When doing cardio work—like sprinting, running, jump rope, jumping jacks, etc.—it's best to breathe in a controlled, steady manner. Avoid panting because that doesn't draw air into your lungs fully and traps stale air in them. That cheats you out of needed Oxygen.

These breathing methods take some practice. But start today and you'll notice improvement in no time!

Part 2: Health & Fitness

Hand Balancing

There aren't many activities that develop your shoulders like hand balancing. I include hand balancing in my workouts at least twice a week. Whether it's handstands, forearm stands, donkey kicks, frog to handstand, or handstand pushups, hand balancing is a great—and fun!—way to work your forearms, shoulders, arms, and core!

You'll also realize that hand balancing improves your overall balance and sense of physical presence. It teaches you to pay attention to signals from muscles and nerves that you wouldn't normally. That translates into better body control and awareness.

If you want to test this principle, take an activity—something you've never done before—and learn it with your weak hand—only practice it on your weak side. Once you've learned to do it with your weak hand, give it a try on the strong side. You'll find you can do it with ease!

Your brain automatically translates information from your weak side to your strong side. The same principle works with your sense of balance. The skills you gain from hand balancing improve your balance while standing or running, etc.

If you want strong shoulders, a solid core, and better balance, throw some handstands or one of my favorites, Donkey Kicks, into your workout routine.

Live a Fitness Lifestyle!

Have you ever wanted to do something but couldn't because you weren't in good enough shape?

That's frustrating isn't it?

The great news is no matter your current fitness level, you can improve! Start today. Choose fitness as a lifestyle.

One of the best things about making fitness a lifestyle is it allows you to do physical activities than you couldn't otherwise. A healthy, fit body is also functions better. It gives you a higher quality of life all around.

You can push yourself harder and do more than people who aren't fit. A healthy, physically fit body can take more and bounce back easier. And, if you're in good shape, most activities won't leave you exhausted.

So if you like outdoor activities, from gardening to rock climbing, if you want to play with your kids, if you enjoy recreational sports, or even if you want to do something a little crazy, Like Batmanning, there's no better way to prepare yourself—and make these activities more enjoyable—than by exercising regularly!

Use Your Legs!

Want a quick workout to burn calories and get your heart pumping?

The biggest muscles groups in your body are in your legs. When those muscles demand oxygen and nutrition—during a workout—your heart beats overtime to get them the blood they need.

What does that mean?

If you want to burn calories and work your heart, the best place to start is with your legs. And if you want to combine your strength and cardio training the best way to get your heart pumping is to start with leg work.

Try a workout like this on for size (**Rest for 30 seconds between sets**):

1 set Hindu Squats x 50
1 set Wrestlers Bridge x 1 minute
1 set Hindu Pushups x 30
1 set Pull-ups x 10
1 set Bicycle Crunches x 50
1 set Font Bridge x 1 minute
1 set Handstand Hold 30 seconds
1 set Hindu Jumping Squats x 10

When you're done, see what you heart and lungs are doing!

*These exercises are described in detail on my Bodyweight Exercise List page.

http://www.rolandbyrd.co/bodyweight-exercise-list/

Part 2: Health & Fitness

Are You in a Fitness Rut?

When you train regularly, there will probably be times you'll get in a rut. Times when it seems, that no matter what you do, you aren't making progress. This isn't as noticeable for those who work out to stay in shape as it is for those seeing size, strength, endurance, or speed gains, but it can still happen. Sometimes it manifests as a physical plateau. Sometimes it shows as a mental block. Sometimes it's an inner voice saying, "You really don't need to work out today..."

Regardless how it manifests, it must be dealt with and quickly!

The best way to fight mental or physical plateaus is by introducing change into your routine. Mix things up. Your body and mind like variety, they like being challenged! When you stick to one workout for too long it can become mundane and your body—being the amazing machine it is—figures out exactly how much it needs to give you to maintain that routine. That's when progress slows and often halts.

But when you shock it by changing things up it says, "Wooah! I'd better figure out how to deal with this!" It does that by improving, by growing stronger, faster, leaner, or building endurance!

Your mind is the same way. When you stop challenging it, it begins to atrophy. That leads to less motivation and makes working out a chore instead of a gift! A new workout is not only a challenge to your body, it creates new neural-

Another Slice of Pi

pathways as your mind and body "Learn" how to do the new movements.

So how do you break through mental and physical plateaus?

Here are a couple of ways:

- Mix up the order of the exercises.
- Change the time of day you exercise.
- Change out some of the exercises with new ones.
- Change the position of your hands or feet when doing the exercise.
- Try a new exercise routine.
- Change the rest time between exercises—a slight increase or decrease can make worlds of difference.
- Find an exercise partner, someone with similar fitness goals. You'll motivate each other!
- Switch from isolation movements to combination movements or the other way around
- Learn a new sport.
- Ask yourself, "Why is fitness important to me?" Then seek exercises that help you achieve that goal!

Remember, if you discover you're getting stale in your workouts, try some of the ideas above. You'll get back on track in no time

Thank you for reading, *Another Slice of Pi!*

If *you enjoyed this book*, please leave a review online and tell your friends!

Visit Roland's Website

http://www.RolandByrd.co/

More Books by Roland:

http://www.rolandbyrd.co/books-by-roland-byrd/

Roland on Twitter:

http://www.Twitter.com/RolandByrd

Roland on Google Plus:

http://bit.ly/RolandByrdG-Plus

Ready to *Change Your Life*?

Enroll in Life 180 University *Today* and *Discover*:

- Exactly how to identify and change problem areas in your life.
- How to use your subconscious mind to help you change.
- How to create a life-long habit of excellence.
- How to discover and become the best you.
- And best of all, how to make these changes last!

http://www.180-u.com

More Books By Roland Byrd:

Your Blueprint, Life by Design
The Pi of Life
Reflections
A Slice of Madness
Break Your Mold
Break Your Mold The Workbook
Break Your Mold Celebration and Success Journal
*The Prosperity Factor with Joe Vitale
The Law of Action

Available From:
    http://www.rolandbyrd.co/books-by-roland-byrd/
    http://amazon.com/author/rolandbyrd

*Roland is a contributing author to this book

Hire Roland to Speak for Your Organization or at Your Event:

http://www.rolandbyrd.co/roland-speaks/

Roland Byrd is the author of seven personal development and transformational books, contributing author to the bestselling book *The Prosperity Factor*—with Joe Vitale, and the founder of *Life 180 University*. His passion is helping people unlock their true power, be their best selves, and master their destiny.

You Want Roland at Your Event!

Roland presents with passion, humor, and energy. He engages his audience and is easy to understand. He uses analogies, stories from his own life, and real-world examples to drive home the principles he teaches.

Book Roland for Your Event Today!
http://www.rolandbyrd.co/roland-speaks/

www.ingramcontent.com/pod-product-compliance
Lightning Source LLC
Chambersburg PA
CBHW031946070426
42453CB00007BA/354